The historic Jesus

David Smith

THE HISTORIC JESUS

BY THE SAME AUTHOR

THE DAYS OF HIS FLESH
Cloth, net, 10s. 6d.

MAN'S NEED OF GOD
Crown 8vo, cloth, 6s.

CHRISTIAN COUNSEL
Crown 8vo, cloth, 5s.

THE FEAST OF THE COVENANT
Crown 8vo, cloth, 3s. 6d.

A LEGEND OF BETHLEHEM
Illustrated in Colour, net, 1s.

A LEGEND OF JERUSALEM
Illustrated in Colour, net, 1s.

LONDON: HODDER AND STOUGHTON

THE HISTORIC JESUS

BEING THE ELLIOTT LECTURES
DELIVERED IN THE WESTERN THEO-
LOGICAL SEMINARY, PITTSBURG, PA.

BY THE REV.

DAVID SMITH, M.A., D.D.

PROFESSOR OF THEOLOGY IN THE MCCREA
MAGEE COLLEGE, LONDONDERRY

HODDER AND STOUGHTON

LONDON   NEW YORK   TORONTO

TO THE

PROFESSORS AND STUDENTS

OF THE WESTERN THEOLOGICAL SEMINARY, PITTSBURG,

AND ALL THE FRIENDS WHO MADE MY FIRST VISIT

TO AMERICA A PLEASANT EXPERIENCE

AND A FRAGRANT MEMORY

1-5 204 536

PREFACE

THE question of the historicity of the evangelic narratives is more than academic; and so I have endeavoured to eschew technicalities and make my argument intelligible to those who, unversed in the science of criticism, are yet troubled by its pronouncements. In truth it is less an argument than a personal confession. It indicates the path by which my own mind has travelled, and my hope is that it may help others to a braver faith in our Lord Jesus Christ.

D. S.

4, THE COLLEGE,
    LONDONDERRY.

CONTENTS

THE CRITICAL CONTENTION

'They have taken away my Lord, and I know not where they have laid Him'

ST. MARY MAGDALENE.

I

THE CRITICAL CONTENTION

AT the outset of his work on *The Agreement of the Evangelists*, ere addressing himself to his proper task of discussing the discrepancies of the fourfold narrative, St. Augustine deals with a preliminary and more vital problem. 'It is needful,' he says, ' first to discuss that question which is wont to disturb not a few: why the Lord wrote nothing Himself, so that it is necessary to believe the writings of others regarding Him. This is said by those, mostly pagans, who dare not impeach or blaspheme the Lord Jesus Christ Himself, and attribute to Him a most excellent wisdom—only, however, as a man; but His disciples, they say, attributed to their Master more than He was; insomuch that they said He was the Son of God, and the Word of God by which all things were made, and He and

Jesus known only by the report of believers.

God the Father were one, and all else of like sort in the apostolic literature whereby we have learned that He should be worshipped as God one with the Father. For they deem that He should be honoured as a most wise man; but that He should be worshipped as God they deny.'

And their contention was by no means irrational. What they conceived to have happened in the case of our Lord has frequently happened in the evolution of religion.

Hero-
worship.

'How the man Odin,' says Carlyle,* 'came to be considered a *god*, the chief god ?—that surely is a question which nobody would wish to dogmatise upon. I have said, his people knew no *limits* to their admiration of him; they had as yet no scale to measure admiration by. Fancy your own generous heart's-love of some greatest man expanding till it *transcended* all bounds, till it filled and overflowed the whole field of your thought ! . . . And then consider what mere Time will do in such cases; how if a man was great while living, he becomes tenfold greater when dead. What an enormous *camera-obscura* magnifier is Tradition ! How a thing

* *On Heroes : The Hero as Divinity.*

grows in the human Memory, in the human Imagination, when love, worship and all that lies in the human Heart, is there to encourage it. And in the darkness, in the entire ignorance; without date or document, no book, no Arundel-marble; only here and there some dumb monu-mental cairn. Why, in thirty or forty years, were there no books, any great man would grow *mythic*, the contemporaries who had seen him being once all dead.'

And so it happened in the case of Jesus according to those early critics, ' mostly pagans,' who were no wanton blasphemers but earnest men, willing to do all justice to Christianity yet refusing to recog-nise a miracle where a natural expla-nation would suffice. It was a reasonable con-tention, and its reasonableness is proved by this —that it has held its ground and is maintained in our own day with stronger cogency and greater persuasiveness. The Jesus of the Gospels, it is alleged, is not the Jesus of history. The picture which the Evangelists have painted is not portraiture but idealisation. It depicts our Lord, not as He actually was in the days of His flesh, but as He appeared to

The evangelic picture not portraiture but idealisation.

a later generation, glorified by reverence and magnified by superstition.

The transformation was effected mainly by the operation of two causes. One was the Messianic expectation of the Jewish people. 'The Messianic time,' says Strauss, anticipating much that has since been written,* 'was expected generally as a time of signs and wonders. The eyes of the blind should be opened, the ears of the deaf should be unstopped, the lame should leap, and the tongue of the dumb extol God.† This, in the first instance quite figuratively intended, was soon understood literally,‡ and hereby the figure of the Messiah, ere ever Jesus appeared, was always sketched more in detail. Thus many of the tales regarding Jesus had not to be newly invented, but had only to be transferred to Jesus from the figure of the Messiah living in the people's hope, into which, with manifold transformations, they had come from the Old Testament, and to be harmonised with his personality

margin note: Two transforming influences:

(1) the Messianic expectation;

---

* *Leb. Jes., Einleit.*, p. 92 f.
† Isa. xxxv. 5 f., xlii. 7 ; cf. xxxii. 3, 4.
‡ Matt. xi. 5 ; Luke vii. 21 f.

and teaching. And so it could never have been easier for the man who introduced such a trait into the description of Jesus, to believe himself that it actually belonged to him, in accordance with the following syllogism: So and so must have happened to the Messiah; Jesus was the Messiah; therefore that will have happened to him.' Given the belief that Jesus was the Messiah, then it was inevitable that the Messianic programme should be assigned to Him. Whatever the Messiah was to be or do, that Jesus must have been and done. And thus prophecy became history.

But even apart from the Messianic Hope the transformation was inevitable. The Evangelists wrote at least a generation after the events which they record, and they beheld and interpreted the past in the light of the present. And what followed? It has been stated thus: 'To realise that the central materials of the gospels were mainly drawn up and collected during the three or four decades which followed the death of Jesus, and that the gospels themselves were not composed until the period 65–105; to realise these facts will show—(i.) that the gospels are not purely

(2) the view-point of a later generation.

objective records, no mere chronicles of pure crude fact, or of speeches preserved verbatim; (ii.) that they were compiled in and for an age when the church required Christ not as a memory so much as a religious standard, and when it reverenced him as an authority for its ideas and usages; (iii.) that they reflect current interests and feelings, and are shaped by the experience and for the circumstances of the church; (iv.) that their conceptions of Christ and Christianity are also moulded to some extent by the activity and expansion of the church between 30 and 60, by its tradition, oral and written, and by its teaching, especially that of Paul.'*

Thus the task of criticism is to work back from the evangelic idealisation to the historic The task of reality, and discover the actual Jesus criticism. by divesting Him of those alien wrappings, unearthing Him from those legendary accumulations, and clearing away the mist which has gathered round Him and hidden Him from view. And the question is: What remains after the work has been accomplished?

* Moffatt, *Hist. N. T.*, p. 45, n. 2.

It has been answered with frank precision by Professor Schmiedel of Zürich in his cataclysmic article on the *Gospels* in the *Encyclopædia Biblica*. There the test of his- toricity is first of all defined on this wise: 'When a profane historian finds before him a historical document which testifies to the worship of a hero unknown to other sources, he attaches first and foremost importance to those features which cannot be deduced from the fact of this worship, and he does so on the simple and sufficient ground that they would not be found in this source unless the author had met with them as fixed data of tradition.' And what is the residuum of historic material after the application of this test to the evangelic narratives? Only nine fragments, a series of negations, emphatic repudiations of supernatural attributes and miraculous powers:

The test of historicity.

The historic residuum

1. Our Lord's answer to the Young Ruler: 'Why callest thou Me good? None is good save one, even God.' *

2. His saying to the Pharisees that 'blas- phemy against the Son of Man can be for- given.' †

---

* Mark x. 17 f.   † Matt. xii. 31 f.

3. The supposition of His relations that He was 'beside Himself.'*

4. His saying: 'Of that day or that hour knoweth no one, not even the angels in heaven, neither the Son, but the Father.'†

5. His cry on the Cross: 'My God, My God, why hast Thou forsaken Me?'‡

6. His refusal of a sign to that generation. §

7. The statement that He 'was able to do no mighty work (save healing a few sick folk) in Nazareth, and marvelled at the unbelief of its people.'‖

8. His warning to the disciples after the miracles of the loaves and fishes,¶ which proves, it is alleged, that the feeding of the multitudes was not a historical occurrence, but a parable having this as its point, that the bread with which one man in the wilderness was able to feed a vast multitude signifies the teaching with which he satisfied their souls.

9. His answer to the messengers of John the

---

* Mark iii. 21. Keim (*Jes. von Naz.*, iii. p. 181, E.T.), on the contrary, discredits this passage, and suggests that it may be derived from 2 Cor. v. 13 ; Acts xxv. 24.

† Mark xiii. 32.   ‡ Mark xv. 34.

§ Mark viii. 12.   ‖ Mark vi. 5 f.

¶ Mark viii. 14–21.

Baptist :* 'The blind receive their sight, and the lame walk, the lepers are cleansed, and the deaf hear, and the dead are raised up, and the poor have the Gospel preached to them'— the last clause counteracting the preceding enumeration and proving that Jesus was speaking not of the physically but of the spiritually blind, lame, leprous, deaf, dead.

These fragments Schmiedel pronounces 'absolutely credible,' 'the foundation-pillars for a truly scientific life of Jesus.' And this is all that is left—this shattered remnant of that precious heritage, the Evangelic Tradition, 'the fairest memorial,' as Weizsäcker terms it,† 'which the primitive Church has raised in its own honour.'

It is hardly possible to exaggerate the seriousness of the issue. The foundation of the Church's faith and hope is her Lord Jesus Christ, according to the ancient definition,‡ 'God of God, Light of Light, very God of very God; begotten, not made; of one essence with the

The seriousness of the issue.

* Matt. xi. 5 ; Luke vii. 22.
† *Urchristenthum*, p. 696.
‡ Creed of Constantinople.

Father; through whom all things were made; who for us men and for our salvation descended from heaven, and was made flesh of the Holy Spirit and the Virgin Mary, and became man; was crucified for us under Pontius Pilate, and suffered, and was buried, and rose again on the third day, according to the Scriptures; and ascended into heaven, and sitteth at the right hand of the Father; and cometh again with glory to judge quick and dead: of whose Kingdom there shall be no end.' All this she believes on the testimony of the Evangelists; and if it be proved that their testimony is a dream, then her faith is whistled down the wind. 'Christ, it is true,' says Bishop Martensen,* 'is not present in the Scriptures alone; it is true, the image of Christ lives in a manner relatively independent of Scripture, in the heart of the Church, and in the heart of each individual believer; but the inward Christ of the heart presupposes the Christ manifested in history, and without the latter soon fades into a mystic cloud. The manifold representations of Christ which exist in the Christian Church as a whole, in the various confessions and sects,

* *Christian Dogmatics*, pp. 239 f.

in the various forms of Christian art and science, all spring from the one grand fundamental form which is sketched in the Gospels; and they must all be judged and tested thereby. If we had not such a representation, no really essential feature of which is absent or incorrect; if Christ were simply the half-apocryphal person to which one-sided critics love to reduce Him, by enveloping Him in an impenetrable mist; we must give up speaking of a Christian revelation in the sense that Christ Himself is its fundamental feature.'

It has, however, been maintained that the disaster is not inevitable. A way of escape has been sought along the line of Green's way the Hegelian philosophy; and by no of escape one has it been more persuasively commended than by that brilliant teacher, the late Mr. T. H. Green of Oxford, the prototype of Langham in Mrs. Humphry Ward's *Robert Elsmere*.

His argument is that it matters not at all whether the evangelic portraiture of Jesus be historical. In point of fact it is not sufficiency of historical. It is a beautiful ideal, the the ideal, creation partly of St. Paul, but still more of one even greater—'the writer whom the church calls St. John.' 'More, probably, than two generations after St. Paul had gone to his rest, there arose a disciple, whose very name we know not (for he sought not his own glory and preferred to hide it under the repute of another), who gave that final spiritual interpretation to the person of Christ, which has for ever taken it out of the region of history and of the doubts that surround all past events, to fix it in the purified conscience as the immanent God.'* Wherefore inquire after the historic Jesus? It is sufficient that this perfect ideal of the relation between God and man has dawned on the world, and it matters neither whence it came nor how it arose.

immateriality of historic evidence.

The thought which Green would here enforce is expressed by Browning in these familiar lines:†

'Ye know there needs no second proof with good
  Gained for our flesh from any earthly source :
  We might go freezing, ages,—give us fire,
  Thereafter we judge fire at its full worth,
  And guard it safe through every chance, ye know !

---

* Green's *Works*, iii. p. 242.
† *A Death in the Desert.*

That fable of Prometheus and his theft,
How mortals gained Jove's fiery flower, grows old
(I have been used to hear the pagans own)
And out of mind ; but fire, howe'er its birth,
Here is it, precious to the sophist now
Who laughs the myth of Æschylus to scorn,
As precious to those satyrs of his play,
Who touched it in gay wonder at the thing.'

It is sufficient that the idea is here ; and indeed it is an impure sort of faith which concerns itself about historic evidence. 'It is not on any estimate of evidence, correct or incorrect, that our true holiness can depend. Neither if we believe certain documents to be genuine and authentic, can we be the better, nor if we believe not, the worse. There is thus an inner contradiction in that conception of faith which makes it a state of mind involving peace with God and love towards all men, and at the same time makes its object that historical work of Christ, of which our knowledge depends on evidence of uncertain origin and value.'*

According to this argument it is in the idea alone that all the value lies. The Objections: history which enshrines it is mere scaffolding, a needless encumbrance once the

* Green's *Works*, iii. p. 260.

structure is complete. It may seem an easy and effective solution, facilitating our disembarrassment and lifting our faith to a secure and serene vantage-ground; yet it is beset by insurmountable difficulties.

One is that it imputes to the Apostles an alien attitude, and an attitude, more-

(1) the Apostles built upon a historic basis.

over, which they expressly repudiate. Christianity was for them no mere idea. It rested on a historic basis.

It is true that St. Paul says to the Corinthians that, 'though he had known Christ after

St. Paul.

the flesh, yet now he knew Him so no more';* but this means that Christ was for him more than a historic personage. He was the Living Lord—

'No dead fact stranded on the shore
    Of the oblivious years;—

'But warm, sweet, tender, even yet
    A present help is he;
And faith has still its Olivet,
    And love its Galilee.'

He was far from rejecting the historic basis or regarding it as unimportant. What does he

* 2 Cor. v. 16.

say when he recapitulates to the Corinthians the Gospel which he had preached unto them, which also they had received; wherein also they stood, by which also they were saved? 'I delivered unto you first of all that which also I received, how that Christ died for our sins according to the Scriptures; and that He was buried; and that He hath been raised on the third day according to the Scriptures; and that He appeared to Cephas; then to the Twelve; then He appeared to above five hundred brethren at once, of whom the greater part remain until now, but some are fallen asleep; then He appeared to James; then to all the Apostles; and last of all, as unto one born out of due time, He appeared to me also.'* The Death and the Resurrection of Jesus were the theme of St. Paul's preaching, and these were historic facts attested by the evidence of eye-witnesses. It is simply flying in the face of his explicit testimony to assert that 'there is no reason to think that he knew anything of the details of the life of Jesus of Nazareth.'

And as for St. John, his theme is not a subjective idea of the immanence of God in

* 1 Cor. xv. 3–8.

man, but an objective revelation enacted on the stage of history. 'The Word,' he says in his Prologue, 'was made flesh, and dwelt among us (and we beheld His glory, glory as of the Only Begotten from the Father), full of grace and truth.' And he begins his first Epistle, which is, in Lightfoot's phrase, a 'commendatory postscript' to his Gospel, with an elaborate assurance that the Incarnation was an actual and historic fact. 'That which was from the beginning, that which we have heard, that which we have seen with our eyes, and our hands handled concerning the Word of life (and the life was manifested, and we have seen, and bear witness, and declare unto you the life, the eternal life, which was with the Father, and was manifested unto us); that which we have seen and heard declare we unto you also, that ye also may have fellowship with us.'

St. John.

Thus, while faith was indeed for St. Paul and St. John 'a state of mind involving peace with God and love towards all men,' it rested for them both on 'the historical work of Christ.'

Moreover, in his attempt to save Christianity

Green sacrifices it. He resolves it into a meta-physical idea, 'the worship, through love and knowledge, of God as a spiritual being immanent in the moral life of man.'* This, however, is not Christianity, nor is it even religion. 'A religion,' says Coleridge,† 'that is a true religion, must consist of ideas and facts both; not of ideas alone without facts, for then it would be mere Philosophy;—nor of facts alone without ideas of which these facts are the symbols, or out of which they arise, or upon which they are grounded, for then it would be mere History.'

(2) A Christianity of ideas without facts not a Gospel but a philosophy,

The truth is that the Christianity of Green is a mere phantom, and whatever be its speculative validity, it has nothing of the efficacy of a Gospel. 'Logicians,' it has been said,‡ 'may reason about abstractions. But the great mass of men must have images. . . . The history of the Jews is the record of a continued struggle between pure Theism, supported by the most terrible sanc-

inefficacious with the multitude.

* Green's *Works*, p. 215.
† *Table Talk*, December 3, 1831.
‡ Macaulay, *Essay on Milton*.

tions, and the strangely fascinating desire of having some visible and tangible object of adoration. Perhaps none of the secondary causes which Gibbon has assigned for the rapidity with which Christianity spread over the world, while Judaism scarcely ever acquired a proselyte, operated more powerfully than this feeling. God, the uncreated, the incomprehensible, the invisible, attracted few worshippers. A philosopher might admire so noble a conception: but the crowd turned away in disgust from words which presented no image to their minds. It was before Deity embodied in a human form, walking among men, partaking of their infirmities, leaning on their bosoms, weeping over their graves, slumbering in the manger, bleeding on the cross, that the prejudices of the Synagogue, and the doubts of the Academy, and the pride of the Portico, and the fasces of the Lictor, and the swords of thirty legions, were humbled in the dust.'

> ' And so the Word had breath, and wrought
>   With human hands the creed of creeds
>   In loveliness of perfect deeds,
> More strong than all poetic thought;

'Which he may read that binds the sheaf,
  Or builds the house, or digs the grave,
  Or those wild eyes that watch the wave
In roarings round the coral reef.'

APOCRYPHAL IDEALISATIONS

'Look here, upon this picture, and on this.'

SHAKSPEARE.

II

APOCRYPHAL IDEALISATIONS

THE critical contention with which we have to do is that the evangelic portraiture of Jesus is unhistorical. It Recapitulation. depicts Him, not as He actually was in the days of His flesh, but as He appeared to the faith of the Church in the succeeding generation; and all His worshipful attributes are merely so much *Aberglaube*. And we have seen how ruinous is the issue. If that contention be allowed, then the Church has been bereft of her Lord. Jesus, so far as He can be known —if indeed He can be known at all—was no Divine Saviour; and all down the centuries the Church has been lavishing her faith and adoration on a creation of her own fancy.

And there is no evasion of the issue. The sole foundation of the Faith is the Historic Jesus, and the Gospels are the only sources of

our knowledge of Him. If they fail us, He is irrecoverably lost.

Our need, then, is to reassure ourselves of the trustworthiness of the evangelic records, that we may enjoy the certainty that their testimony is true, exhibiting our Lord as He appeared to the eyes of His contemporaries ; and to this end my purpose is, not to deal with the intricate and fascinating problems of New Testament Criticism, but to pursue a line of argument which, it seems to me, is at once simple and effective, instituting a comparison between the evangelic portraiture as it stands and the pictures which the devout imagination of the second century produced.   And when we have seen what idealisation has actually accomplished, it will then appear whether it be conceivable that the evangelic portraiture is a product of the same process.

Our line of argument: comparison of Gospels with actual idealisations.

For this purpose there lies to hand a sufficiency of material. Our Evangelists are not, in the proper sense, biographers of Jesus, forasmuch as they do not narrate the full story of His earthly life. St. Mark and St. John begin with His manifes-

Occasion of idealisation.

tation as the Messiah, and narrate His brief
ministry of only three years' duration; and as
for St. Matthew and St. Luke, they begin
indeed with the story of His Birth, but thereafter, save for that solitary incident which the
diligence of the latter has rescued from oblivion
—the Holy Child's visit to Jerusalem during
the season of the Passover *—there is a long
hiatus of thirty years in their narratives, and
they resume where St. Mark and St. John
begin.

It was inevitable that the mystery of the
Silent Years should excite curiosity, and in the
complete absence of information the *Its preva-*
myth-forming genius of the primitive *lence in the primitive*
Church found its opportunity. It set *Church.*
to work very early. St. Luke has told us that,
ere he composed his Gospel, many others had
essayed the task; and it was their lack of
discrimination that moved him to investigate
the Evangelic Tradition and publish an accu-
rate version of it. † And from the Pastoral
Epistles to Timothy it appears how seriously
the Tradition was imperilled in those days.
It was in danger, on the one hand, of being

* Luke ii. 41–51.　　　† Luke i. 1–4.

mutilated by heretical teachers, 'consenting not to sound words, even those of our Lord Jesus Christ, and to the doctrine which is according to godliness, puffed up, knowing nothing, but doting about questionings and logomachies'; * and, on the other hand, of being corrupted by an admixture of 'profane and oldwifish myths.' † And it was this twofold danger that necessitated the committal of the precious Tradition, 'the genuine deposit,'‡ to a permanent and authoritative record. §

Of this profuse literature, innocent in its intention yet subversive of the very foundations of the Faith, two interesting specimens have survived.

Two specimens:

One is the apocryphal Gospel known as the *Protevangelium Jacobi.* It is the story of Mary, the Mother of our Lord, and it professes to be the work of His brother James. Of course the latter claim is groundless, nevertheless the book is demonstrably very ancient. In his commentary on St. Matthew (c. A.D. 246) Origen refers to it in conjunction with the *Gospel according to*

(1) Prot-evangelium Jacobi,

* 1 Tim. vi. 3, 4.   † 1 Tim. iv. 7.   ‡ 2 Tim. i. 14.
§ Cf. *The Days of His Flesh*, Introd., pp. xv f.

Peter, plainly ranking them together in notoriety and authority.* And the *Gospel according to Peter* is of high antiquity. In his letter to the Church of Rhossos, Serapion, Bishop of Antioch (A.D. 190–203), defends the sanction which he had given to the reading of it in the Church, inasmuch as, notwithstanding Doketic additions, most of it belonged to the right doctrine of the Saviour.† Since time was required for its circulation and recognition, this testimony carries the *Gospel according to Peter*, and with it our *Protevangelium*, well into the second century. Further, the *Protevangelium* is thrice quoted, as though possessed of full authority, by St. Justin Martyr — twice in his *Dialogue with Trypho* (c. A.D. 136),‡ and again in his first

---

* x. 17 : τοὺς δὲ ἀδελφοὺς Ἰησοῦ φασὶ τινες εἶναι, ἐκ παραδόσεως ὁρμώμενοι τοῦ ἐπιγεγραμμένου κατὰ Πέτρον εὐαγγελίου ἢ τῆς βίβλου Ἰακώβου, υἱοὺς Ἰωσὴφ ἐκ προτέρας γυναικὸς συνῳκηκυίας αὐτῷ πρὸ τῆς Μαρίας.

† Euseb., *H. E.*, vi. 12.

‡ *Dial.* 78 (Jesus born in a cave near Bethlehem) : ἐπειδὴ Ἰωσὴφ οὐκ εἶχεν ἐν τῇ κώμῃ ἐκείνῃ ποῦ καταλῦσαι, ἐν σπηλαίῳ τινὶ σύνεγγυς τῆς κώμης κατέλυσε· καὶ τότε αὐτῶν ὄντων ἐκεῖ ἐτετόκει ἡ Μαρία τὸν Χριστόν. Cf. *Protev.* xviii. *Dial.* 100 . χαρὰν λαβοῦσα Μαρία ἡ παρθένος εὐαγγελιζομένου Γαβριὴλ ἀγγέλου. Cf. *Protev.* xii. 2 : χαρὰν δὲ λαβοῦσα Μαριὰμ ἀπίει πρὸς Ἐλισάβετ.

Apology, addressed to Antoninus Pius (c. A.D. 146).* It could hardly have acquired such recognition in less than a generation, and this carries it back to the beginning of the second century.†

(2) *Evangelium Thomæ.*

The other book which claims our attention is the *Evangelium Thomæ,* and its antiquity can scarcely be less, since it is quoted, though in terms of reprobation, by St. Irenæus in his great work on *Heresies* (A.D. 182–188).‡

Whatever be the precise date of these two apocrypha, they originated in the period which, it is contended, produced the evangelic portraiture of Jesus; and it is thus legitimate to compare their representation with it, and judge whether they belong to the same order in respect of historicity.

---

* *Apol.* i. 33 : ἰδοὺ συλλήψει ἐν γαστρὶ ἐκ Πνεύματος Ἁγίου, καὶ τέξει υἱὸν, καὶ Υἱὸς Ὑψίστου κληθήσεται· καὶ καλέσεις τὸ ὄνομα Ἰησοῦν· αὐτὸς γὰρ σώσει τὸν λαὸν αὐτοῦ ἀπὸ τῶν ἁμαρτιῶν αὐτῶν. Similarly *Protev.* xi. (1) substitutes Υἱὸς Ὑψίστου for Υἱὸς Θεοῦ (Luke i. 35), and (2) includes in the Annunciation to Mary the angel's words to Joseph (Matt. i. 21). It is evident that St. Justin had the *Protevangelium* before him.

† Cf. Tischendorf, *Ev. Apocr.,* pp. xii ff., xxxviii f. ; Zahn, *N. T. Kan.,* i. 914 f., ii. 774 ff.

‡ I. xiii. 1. Cf. *Ev. Thom.* vi.

The *Protevangelium* is a *Tendenzschrift*, and it is dominated by a twofold apologetic purpose, being directed, in the first place, Twofold purpose of Protevangelium : against the Doketic heresy which was maintained by Cerinthus, the contemporary of the Apostle John at Ephesus,* that Jesus was the son of Joseph and Mary by ordinary generation, and, moreover, against the Jewish calumny that He was the illegitimate offspring of Mary and the soldier Panthera.†

It meets the former by representing Joseph as a widower of great age when he was entrusted with the guardianship of Mary. against Doketic denial of Virgin Birth ; From infancy she had been a ward of the Temple, and she was not married to Joseph but committed to his care when she attained the age of twelve years, 'lest she should defile the Sanctuary of the Lord.' He was reluctant to undertake the charge. 'I have sons,' he remonstrated, 'and I am an old man, and she is a girl. I shall become a laughing-stock to the children of Israel.' However, he was overborne by the insistence of the priests and their threat of judgment should he disobey; and so he conveyed her to his house, and went

* Iren. I. xxi.   † Orig., *C. Cels.* i. 28, 32.

abroad in prosecution of his calling, and saw her no more for six months. 'Behold,' he said to her at his departure, 'I received thee from the Temple of the Lord; and now I leave thee in my house and go away to work at my buildings, and I shall come back to thee. The Lord will keep thee safe.'

And as for the Jewish calumny, this is met by attesting the perpetual virginity of Mary.

Against Jewish calumniation of Mary. It is related, with somewhat unsavoury elaboration, how she brought forth the Holy Child *salva virginitate*, and Salome's hand was blasted when she would not credit the midwife's story without such tangible evidence as Thomas craved of the reality of the Resurrection.* And Mary's virginity remained, for the brethren of Jesus were not her children but the fruit of Joseph's former marriage.

All this stands in striking contrast to the stories of the Birth of Jesus in the Gospels *Contrast with the Gospels.* according to St. Matthew and St. Luke. The distinction of the latter lies in their fearlessness, their freedom from apologetic solicitude. The Evangelists must

* John xx. 25.

have been aware what would be said, what
actually had been and was being said, of
the Virgin Birth; yet they evince no con-
cern to safeguard the story and obviate mis-
construction. They report it simply as they
had it from the lips of their informants, who
would seem from internal evidence to have
been no other than Joseph and Mary; and
they never attempt to buttress it by legendary
accretions. There is not a touch of the gro-
tesque in their narratives.

The explanation is certainly not that they
were superior to their apocryphal rival in
literary instinct and æsthetic discrimi- Reason of the
nation, and disdained the 'profane and difference:
oldwifish myths' in which he revelled. not artistic
For in truth he was no mean artist. the Gospels,
There is hardly anything in early literature
more impressive than the passage where he
describes how at the moment of the Saviour's
birth a hush fell upon creation, and all things,
animate and inanimate, paused as in amazement
and adoration. Mary had found a shelter, and
Joseph had gone forth in quest of succour, when
suddenly the wonder befell. 'I walked,' he
says, 'and I walked not. And I looked up

to the air, and I saw the air astonied.   And
I looked up to the vault of heaven, and I saw
it standing still and the fowls of heaven keeping
quiet. And I looked upon the earth, and I
saw a dish set and labourers at their meat, and
their hands were in the dish; and they that
were chewing chewed not, and they that were
lifting their morsel brought it not up, and they
that were putting it to their mouth put it
not, but all their faces were looking up. And
I saw sheep being driven, and the sheep stood
still; and the shepherd lifted his hand to smite
them, and his hand stopped up. And I looked
upon the stream of the river, and I saw the
mouths of the kids laid unto it and not drink-
ing.   And all things for the moment were
driven from their course.'

This is a fine imagination, worthy of Dante
or Raphael, and comparable with that other

but their
historic
faithfulness

legend that, when the Saviour died
on the Cross, every green thing in
the world withered. It was not for
lack of art that the writer failed, but rather for
this—that he attempted the impossible task of
dealing imaginatively with the supernatural.
The fiction of that ethereal personage, the

White Lady of Avenel, is a fatal blot upon
the tale of *The Monastery*, and Sir Walter
acknowledged the justice of the disfavour with
which it was received, and pleaded only the
extreme difficulty of managing the machinery
of the supernatural.* It is indeed an impossible
achievement, and as Sir Walter failed, so did
the author of the *Protevangelium* before him.
And how did it come to pass that, where others
with every resource of genius and art have dis-
astrously failed, our Evangelists have so con-
spicuously succeeded? The reason is simply
this—that they were not creators but historians;
they were not dealing imaginatively with the
supernatural but reporting an actual manifestation, ἡ τοῦ Σωτῆρος ἡμῶν Ἰησοῦ Χριστοῦ ἔνσαρκος
οἰκονομία.

Turn now to the *Evangelium Thomæ*. It is
a tissue of Doketic legends of the
Child Jesus, and it depicts Him as Doketism of
a veritable *Wunderkind*. *Evangelium Thomæ:*

* Cf. Horace's counsel concerning the *Deus ex machina*
(*A. P.* 191 f.):

   'Nec deus intersit nisi dignus vindice nodus
   Inciderit.'

(1) Even in those early days He was endowed with miraculous power, and
the miracles which He wrought were
of the most startling sort.

(1) miraculous power of the Holy Child;

One Sabbath Day, when He was five years
of age, He was playing by a stream, and He
gathered the running water into pools and
cleared them of mud by a word of command.
Then He made clay and moulded twelve
sparrows. His playmates went and told Joseph
how He was profaning the Sabbath, and Joseph
came and remonstrated with Him; whereupon
the Child clapped His hands and shouted to
the sparrows 'Away!' and off they flew twitter-
ing. The son of Annas the Scribe was standing
by, and he took a branch and broke down the
pools. 'Villain!' cried Jesus, 'impious and
foolish! wherein did the pools and the water
harm thee? Behold, now, thou also shalt be
withered like a tree, and never bear leaves nor
root nor fruit.' And immediately the child was
all withered.

Again, as He was passing through a village,
He was jostled by a boy. This angered Him,
and He said: 'Thou shalt not go thy way';
and the boy fell down and died.

Such, according to this apocryphal legend-monger, was the Boy Jesus—not the sweet child of whom we catch a glimpse in St. Luke's narrative, 'subject unto His parents' and 'advancing in favour with God and men,'* but lawless, passionate, and vindictive, a terror to the neighbours. 'With such a child,' they said to Joseph, 'thou canst not dwell with us in the village; or else teach Him to bless and not to curse; for He kills our children.' But He scorned Joseph's admonition; 'and no one durst anger Him, lest He should curse him, and he should be maimed.' 'And Joseph was grieved, and charged His mother: "Let Him not go out of doors, because those that anger Him die."' Of course this representation stands in glaring contrast to the evangelic narratives. It is in protest against such contemporary legends that St. John observes so pointedly that the miracle at Cana was the first which our Lord ever wrought.† And there is a wide difference between these legendary miracles and the wonderful works which, according to our Evangelists, He wrought during the years of His

* Luke ii. 51, 52.   † John ii. 11.

ministry, when He went about continually doing good,

> 'the shadow of Him Love,
> The speech of Him soft Music, and His step
> A Benediction.'

The evangelic miracles were always works of mercy and compassion; and whatever we may think of their theoretical possibility, our hearts approve them. We would like them to be true, and they 'have our vote to be so if they can.'

(2) As He appears in the *Evangelium Thomæ*, the Holy Child was endowed with superhuman wisdom. He was omniscient in His

(2) His superhuman wisdom.

very cradle. At the age of five years He was sent to school, and His teacher, Zacchæus, repeated the Alphabet to Him from Alpha to Omega. 'Thou hypocrite!' cried the Child, 'when thou knowest not the Alpha according to its nature, how dost thou teach others the Beta?' And then He began to catechise the teacher, and expounded to him the mystical significance of Alpha, after the manner of the Jewish sect of the Cabbalists and the Gnostic sect of the

Marcosians as they appear on the pages of St. Irenæus. Zacchæus was confounded. 'Take Him away, I beseech thee, brother Joseph. I cannot bear the austerity of His look. This Child is not earth-born. Belike He hath been born ere the creation of the world.'

At the age of six years another teacher took Him in hand, and proposed to instruct Him first in Greek and then in Hebrew. Jesus, however, would answer none of his questions. 'If thou art really a teacher,' He said, 'and if thou knowest the letters well, tell Me the force of the Alpha, and I will tell thee that of the Beta.' The exasperated teacher struck Him on the head, and Jesus cursed him and laid him dead on the ground.

Another teacher, a friend of Joseph's, under took the perilous task of His tuition. 'Bring Him to me,' he said; 'perhaps I may be able by dint of flattery to teach Him the letters.' Jesus went to the school, and, finding a book on the desk, took it and would not read its letters, but He opened His mouth and spake by the Holy Spirit and taught the Law to the bystanders. 'I received the Child,' exclaimed the astonished teacher, 'as a disciple, but He is full of much grace and wisdom!' The flattery succeeded. The Child laughed. 'For thy sake,' said He, 'the other teacher who was stricken shall be healed.'

Of course all this is rank Doketism, and it is a denial of the Incarnation. Our Lord in the days of His flesh was not God walking the earth in the semblance of a man; He was the Eternal Son of God become man, and 'in all things made like unto His brethren.'* He was like them in weakness and weariness, and in nescience too; and in His human childhood He 'advanced in wisdom and stature'—a normal growth at once physical and intellectual.

And now consider the bearing of this on the problem of the historicity of the Evangelic Jesus. The point is that the apocry-

Argument for historicity of the Gospels.

phal picture is precisely the sort of idealisation which the imagination of those days must have produced. And this for two reasons. The first is that it was a doctrine of Jewish theology that the Messiah would be a miracle-worker, and would thus attest His

* Heb. ii. 17.

Messiahship. It was on this account that the Pharisees were continually challenging our Lord to show them a sign, that they might believe. And thus it was inevitable that the legend-creators, partly with a deliberate apologetic purpose, partly by the unconscious instinct of faith, should crowd His life with miracles, the more stupendous the better. And then there was the prevailing conception of God, Jewish and Pagan alike, as jealous and vindictive. You remember the Greek motive for humility? 'The Deity,' said Solon,* 'is all envious and troublous,' grudging that mortals should be too happy, and, when they recklessly exulted, smiting and crushing them. Therefore wisdom lay in walking softly, lest one should provoke the divine envy. And similar was the Jewish conception. It was perilous to have to do with Jehovah. Think how the people were warned off from Sinai and bounds were set about the mount, 'lest the Lord should break forth upon them.'† And there is the grim story of Uzzah who, when the Ark was being fetched home from Kirjath-jearim, put forth his hand to steady it on the cart, 'for the oxen shook it.

* Herod. i. 32.   † Exod. xix. 21–24.

And the anger of the Lord was kindled against Uzzah; and God smote him there for his error; and there he died by the Ark of God.'* And you remember the Rabbinical phrase for canonicity? The canonical books were said to 'defile the hands,' the idea being that they were sacred, and handling them lightly was an impiety involving ceremonial uncleanness and demanding ceremonial ablution.† It was in accordance with this principle that the Pharisees inferred from our Lord's miracles of mercy that He was in league with the Devil. Had they been wrought by the power of God, they must needs have been terrible.

Such was the prevailing conception of God, and the evangelic conception was novel, undreamed of, incredible. And this is the argument: If the evangelic portraiture of Jesus were a second-century idealisation, it would be in no wise what it is but precisely the reverse. The Incarnate Son of God would have been conceived, not as a gentle, gracious Friend of Sinners, but as a terrible and wrathful Avenger. And it is even so that He actually appears in those indubitable idealisations.

* 2 Sam. vi. 6–11.
† Cf. Robertson Smith, *O. T. in Jew. Ch.*, p. 173.

RIVALS OF THE EVANGELIC JESUS

ποῦ νῦν τῆς Ἑλλάδος ὁ τῦφος; ποῦ τῶν Ἀθηνῶν τὸ ὄνομα;
ποῦ τῶν φιλοσόφων ὁ λῆρος; ὁ ἀπὸ Γαλιλαίας, ὁ ἀπὸ Βηθσαιδὰ,
ὁ ἄγροικος, πάντων ἐκείνων περιεγένετο

[ST. CHRYSOSTOM, *In Act. Apost. Hom. IV.*

III

RIVALS OF THE EVANGELIC JESUS

FROM those two apocrypha, the *Protevangelium Jacobi* and the *Evangelium Thomæ*, we have learned what the faith of the primitive Church did in the way of Recapitulation. idealising the historic Jesus; and it seems an inevitable inference that the evangelic portraiture cannot possibly be a product of the same process: it is so unlike what the myth-forming genius of those days actually created and, in view of its presuppositions, could not help creating. And now let us pursue the argument along another line.

At the outset of its career Christianity was laughed to scorn by the intellectual world. In the phrase of the Apostle,* it was 'unto the

---

* 1 Cor. i. 23. Cf. the sneer of the philosopher Celsus (Orig., *C. Cels.* iii. 44) at the terms of admission to the Church: 'Let no educated person approach, no wise, no

Greeks foolishness.' Presently, however, this attitude was abandoned. Ere the middle of

Two pagan attitudes to early Christianity.

the second century Christianity had proved itself no mere folly to be laughed at, but a force to be reckoned with; and it was then dealt with after two methods. One was argument, and

(1) argument,

the protagonist was the philosopher Celsus, whose clever attack, *The True Word*, reinforced the Faith by evoking Origen's brilliant apology. The other method was more subtle and elusive. It was the method

(2) rivalry.

to which St. Augustine alludes in that passage which engaged us at the outset. It did not openly assail Christianity, but sought rather to undermine it by proving that whatever was true and beautiful in it was found also no less but even more in Paganism. By a just instinct those champions of the ancient order recognised that there is no Christianity apart from Christ, and they sought to compass its destruction by robbing Him of His unique distinction. Unable and, perhaps, unwilling to deny His excellence, they set themselves not to depreciate

prudent; but if any be illiterate, if any be foolish, if any be uneducated, if any be a babe, let him boldly come.'

but to match it. They painted ideal pictures of prophets of their own, and exhibited those rivals of Jesus, making no mention of Him but allowing the obvious comparison to present itself and suggest the intended inference. They said nothing, but their meaning was: 'See! here is something nobler and wiser than your Galilean.'

Of this method there are extant two conspicuous examples—Lucian's *Life of Demonax* and Philostratus' *Life of Apollonius of Tyana*. Two specimens of the latter

Lucian, that brilliant man of letters, the last of the great Greek writers, was born at Samosata on the Euphrates during the reign of Trajan (A.D. 98–117); and, according to the Byzantine lexicographer, Suidas, he followed the legal profession for a time at Syrian Antioch, but, failing in it, he abandoned it for literature. Suidas says that he was designated 'the Blasphemer,' and that he was torn in pieces by dogs for his madness against the Truth. This notion of him is traditional and still prevails, but it is far from just. In Lucian's Demonax. Lucian's attitude to religion.

those days the ancient religions were at a sorry pass. 'The various modes of worship which prevailed in the Roman world,' says Gibbon in one of his pregnant epigrams,* 'were all regarded by the people as equally true; by the philosopher, as equally false; and by the magistrate, as equally useful.' Religion was a mass of ridiculous and too often immoral superstitions, the jest and scorn of reasonable men; and it is to the credit of Lucian that he would fain have rid humanity of the baleful incubus. It was a blunder, but it was no crime, that, imperfectly acquainted with Christianity, he regarded it as merely the latest phase of the ever-shifting phantasmagoria and pelted it with the artillery of his satire.

His ideal wise man is the eclectic philosopher Demonax, who was born of good parentage in The Greek the island of Cyprus, and taught at spirit. Athens towards the close of the first century and well into the second; and in every feature of his portraiture one recognises a tacit comparison with 'that gibbeted sophist,' as Lucian elsewhere terms our Lord.† What

* *Decline and Fall*, chap. ii.
† *De Mort. Peregr.* 13.

was it in Jesus that chiefly offended the Greek spirit? It was His gravity, His constancy of purpose and His strenuous devotion thereto, so alien from the εὐτραπελία* of the jocund Greeks, so contrary to their maxim μηδὲν ἄγαν, *ne quid nimis*, which Socrates called 'a young man's virtue.'† He took life so seriously, always, as the Greek proverb puts it, 'carrying things to the sweating-point,'‡ and never disarming opposition by a timely jest. It was this temper that involved Him in so many embarrassments, and finally brought Him to the Cross.

To Lucian this seemed the extremity of folly, and he set in contrast the sanity of his Demonax, an eclectic philosopher who The ideal addicted himself to neither of the wise man: dominant and antagonistic schools of his day —the Stoic and the Epicurean—but appropriated the good of both, and regarded the follies of men with an easy and amused tolerance. 'He did not,' says his biographer, 'indulge in the irony of Socrates, but his con-

* The word translated 'jesting' in Eph. v. 4.
† Diog. Laert. ii. 32.
‡ Marc. Antonin. i. 16 : ἕως ἰδρῶτος.

The Historic Jesus   8

versations were full of Attic grace, insomuch
that, when those who had held intercourse
with him went away, they neither despised
him as vulgar nor fled from the churlishness
of his rebukes, but were transported by merri-
ment, and were far more orderly and cheerful,
and had good hope for the future. Never was
he seen crying aloud or straining unduly or
irritated, even when censure was needed; but,
while he was down upon the sins, he had indul-
gence for the sinners, and thought it meet to
take example from the physicians, who, while
they heal the sicknesses, show no anger against
the sick; for he deemed it the part of a god
or a godlike man to correct the error. . . . And
such aid had he from the Graces and Aphrodite
herself in doing and saying all this that, as the
comedy has it, " Persuasion sate ever on his
lips." '

In illustration of this quality in his hero
Lucian produces a collection of his *bons mots*
—caustic criticisms, like his remark
his sanity,
on a futile disputation between two
philosophers, that 'one of them was milking a
he-goat, and the other holding the pail'; or
shrewd precepts, like his answer to a newly-

appointed provincial governor who asked him
how he would govern best: 'Never lose your
temper; talk little; and hear much.' These
things make excellent reading, but it is not for
their own sake that Lucian quotes them. Their
use is to point the underlying contrast between
Jesus and His rival. They exemplify the wise
man's sanity. He was no ascetic, glorifying
poverty, privation, persecution. He appreciated
the good things of life, and held that if a man
were wise, he had the better right to enjoy
them. 'Do you eat sweet cakes?' he was
once asked. 'Yes,' he replied; 'do you suppose it is for the fools that the bees store their
honeycombs?' He had no fancy to play the
martyr needlessly. Once, when he was stepping
into the bath, he shrank back because the water
was too hot, and, being twitted with cowardice,
he retorted: 'Tell me, was it for my country
that I was going to suffer it?' And he made
no preposterous claims to superiority over the
great men of the past. 'Behold,' said Jesus,
'a greater than Solomon is here.'* But once,
when Demonax visited Olympia and the
magistrates proposed to erect a statue in his

* Matt. xii. 42.

honour, 'On no account, gentlemen,' said he. 'Do not reproach your ancestors for not erecting a statue either of Socrates or of Diogenes.'

'Such was the manner of his philosophy— meek, gentle, and blithe'; and the book closes with a description of the peace of his latter days and his passing hence —a charming picture in striking contrast to the tragic close of the Gospel story. 'He lived for nigh a hundred years without sickness, without pain, never troublesome to any nor beholden to any, serviceable to his friends, never having made a single enemy. . . . Unbidden, he would sup and sleep in any house he passed, the inhabitants accounting that it was a visitation of God and a good divinity had entered into their house.' And what did Jesus say? 'The foxes have holes, and the birds of the air have nests; but the Son of Man hath not where to lay His head.'* 'He was despised and rejected of men; a man of sorrows, and acquainted with grief: and as one from whom men hide their face He was despised, and we esteemed Him not.'† When

his felicity.

---

* Matt. viii. 20.   † Isa. liii. 3.

Demonax died the Athenians gave him a public funeral and mourned him long; and the stone seat where he had been wont to rest, they worshipped and wreathed with garlands; and philosophers carried him to his burial. But what of Jesus? 'They plaited a crown of thorns, and put it on His head, and a reed in His right hand; and they kneeled down before Him, and mocked Him, saying, Hail, King of the Jews! And they spat upon Him, and took the reed and smote Him on the head. And when they had mocked Him, they took off from Him the robe, and put on Him His garments, and led Him away to crucify Him.'*

There are the rival pictures, and the heart of humanity has judged between Lucian and the Evangelists. It has chosen the Man of Sorrows, and has found in Him all its salvation and all its desire.

> 'Is it not strange, the darkest hour
> That ever dawn'd on sinful earth
> Should touch the heart with softer power
> For comfort, than an angel's mirth?'

---

* Matt. xxvii. 29–31.

At the first, however, the Man of Sorrows was an offence both to the Jew and to the Greek; and here once more it appears how alien was the evangelic portraiture from the ideal of that generation, how remote from its imagination.

We pass into a different and less wholesome atmosphere when we turn to the consideration of that other rival of the Evangelic Jesus—Apollonius of Tyana. Side by side with the literary movement which had Lucian for its most distinguished representative and which aimed at the suppression of superstition, another movement was in progress during the second century. Its most remarkable phase was the Neo-Pythagoreanism which arose in the reign of Augustus, and which essayed to revive the philosophy of Pythagoras by infusing into it the new life of Oriental theosophy. It is interesting to recall how St. Justin Martyr resorted to a teacher of this school in the course of his long and fruitless search after truth and happiness.*

Philostratus' Apollonius of Tyana.

Neo-Pythagoreanism.

* *Dial. c. Tryph.* 2.

Apollonius, the hero of the somewhat pon-
derous romance which the elder Philostratus
compiled from the memoranda of
Damis of Nineveh at the instance   Apollonius,
of Julia Domna, the Syrian empress of Sep-
timius Severus, was a Neo-Pythagorean. The
story runs that he was born in the same year
as our Lord of an ancient and wealthy family
in the Cappadocian town of Tyana ; and his
birth, like our Lord's, was supernatural, since
he was an incarnation of the Egyptian deity,
the changeful Proteus. He studied a while
at Tarsus, contemporary with Saul the future
Apostle, and then betook himself to the neigh-
bouring town of Ægæ, where he acquired a
knowledge of medicine in the school of the
temple of Asklepios, and embraced Pytha-
goreanism. On the death of his father he
divided his inheritance among his poorer rela-
tives and set out on his travels. He visited
India, and there conversed with the Brahmans
and was initiated into their magical lore. Then
he journeyed westward again, and visited
Greece, Egypt, Rome, and Spain, attended
everywhere by a band of disciples. Wherever
he went he wrought wonders and was revered

as a god. He settled eventually at Ephesus,
where St. John ministered contemporaneously,
and vanished from the earth at the age of nigh
a hundred years, still hale and fresh as a youth.

Philostratus no more than Lucian announces
his purpose of setting up a rival to Jesus, but
a rival of
Jesus.
it was unmistakable and was at once
perceived. About the year 305 there
appeared an anti-Christian work entitled the
Philalethes, now lost and known chiefly by the
replies which it elicited from Eusebius and
Lactantius. Its author was Hierocles, who as
a judge at Nicomedia distinguished himself
by his activity in Diocletian's persecution, and
in recognition of his zeal was promoted to the
governorship of Alexandria. The *Philalethes*
was an elaborate comparison of Jesus and
Apollonius and a demonstration of the latter's
superiority. And the extravagance was repeated by the English Deist, Charles Blount,
who in the year 1680 published a translation
of the first two books of the *Life of Apollonius*
with significant annotations.

Here is an instance of the method of this
covert attack upon our Lord. It is related
that during his sojourn at Rome Apollonius

encountered a funeral procession. A young lady of rank had died, and her bridegroom was attending her remains to the tomb with a numerous retinue of mourners. Apollonius bade them set down the bier and, inquiring the lady's name, took her hand, spoke into her ear, and awoke her from the seeming death. She uttered a cry and returned to her father's house, like Alkestis restored to life by Herakles. It is Damis, the Boswell of Apollonius, who narrates the incident, and he adds: 'Whether it was that he had found a spark of the soul in her which had escaped the notice of the physicians—for it is said that drops of rain fell and she exhaled a vapour from her face—or that he had warmed the extinct soul and recovered it, is beyond the decision alike of me and of the bystanders.' *

Examples of the method: (1) a resurrection at Rome,

There is here plainly a reference to St. Luke's story of the Raising of the Widow's Son at Nain,† and the purpose is to suggest the unreality of our Lord's miracle, after the manner of the rationalistic explanation of the 'raisings from the dead' as merely 'deliverances from premature burial.'

* iv. 45.   † Luke vii. 11–17.

There is indeed much in the story of Apollonius that is admirable and profitable. He
was a powerful preacher, and discoursed excellently to the thronging multitude on mutual
service and public spirit,* wisdom, courage,
temperance,† and other goodly virtues. And
his accustomed formula of prayer is worth
remembering : 'O ye gods, give me the things
that are due.'‡ But there is much also in the
story that is dark and horrible. It is told how
a pestilence had visited Ephesus, and the despairing citizens summoned Apollonius from Smyrna to succour them.

(2) a demoniac at Ephesus.

He assembled them, young and old,
in the theatre, and among them was an
aged beggar, ragged and foul, with blinking
eyes, carrying a wallet with a crust of bread
in it. Apollonius set him in the midst, and
bade the crowd gather stones and pelt the
enemy of the gods. They hesitated, thinking
it a cruel thing to kill a stranger in so miserable
a plight, and pitying the wretch's entreaties.
Apollonius, however, urged them on, and as
the first stones smote him, fire flashed from the

* iv. 3, 8. † iv. 31.
‡ i. 11 : ὦ θεοὶ, δοίητέ μοι τὰ ὀφειλόμενα. Cf. iv. 40.

victim's eyes and the demon was revealed. He was promptly despatched and covered by a hillock of stones. 'Take away the stones,' said Apollonius, 'and discover the wild beast you have killed.' They obeyed, and, behold, the old beggar had vanished, and in his place lay the battered carcase of a hound, huge as the hugest lion, its mouth a-foam like a mad dog's.*

Now we have seen what manner of ideals sprang up and flourished in the imagination of that generation; and —here is the question—is it possible to believe that the Evangelic Jesus is a growth of the same rank soil?

Argument for historicity of the Gospels.

It is told that after the death of the Danish sculptor Thorwaldsen his handiworks were conveyed from his studio at Rome to the museum at Copenhagen, and soon after their arrival there sprang up and bloomed in the courtyard of the museum sweet plants unknown in that northern clime. They were plainly no native products. Whence had they come? The creations of the master had been swathed in

* iv. 10. Cf. *Ev. Infant. Arab.* xxxv, where Satan leaves the child Judas in the form of a mad dog.

straw and grass which had grown on the Roman Campagna, and when the packing-cases were opened the seeds had been scattered and had taken root. Presently the flowers appeared, and there was no mistaking their alien origin.

And it is even so with the evangelic portraiture. It stands unique, unrivalled, *sui generis*, amid the rank growths, the religious, literary, and philosophic imaginations of the second century, proclaiming itself no earth-born dream but a heaven-sent revelation. This is the evidence of its historicity—the impossibility of its imagination by the mind of that generation.

THE SELF-EVIDENCE OF THE
EVANGELIC PORTRAITURE

'THEY dried up all my Jacob's wells;
  They broke the faithful shepherd's rod;
  They blurred the gracious miracles
  Which are the signature of God.

'In trouble, then, and fear I sought
  The Man who taught in Galilee,
  And peace unto my soul was brought,
  And all my faith came back to me.

'Oh times of weak and wavering faith
  That labour pleas in His defence,
  Ye only dim Him with your breath:
  He is His own best evidence.'

                    WALTER C. SMITH.

IV

THE SELF-EVIDENCE OF THE EVANGELIC PORTRAITURE

IN the opening chapter of the Fourth Gospel, which tells the story of the Messiah's manifestation unto Israel at Bethany beyond Jordan, it is written how Philip, in the wonder and joy of his great discovery, sought out Nathanael and told him the glad tidings. 'Him,' he cried, jerking it out in disjointed eagerness, 'whom Moses in the Law wrote of, and the Prophets, we have found—Jesus—the son of Joseph—the man from Nazareth!' Nathanael would not believe it. Himself a Galilean, he knew the ignorance of the northern province and the evil reputation of that rude town. 'Out of Nazareth,' said he disdainfully, 'can there be anything good?' Philip eschewed argument, preferring a surer

The sight of Jesus convincing in the days of His flesh.

way. He answered simply : ' Come and see.
They went to Jesus, and presently Nathanael's
incredulity was conquered, and his heart leaped
up in adoring recognition. ' Rabbi,' he cried,
' Thou art the Son of God, Thou art the King
of Israel ! '

And it was ever thus with those who approached Jesus in the days of His flesh. He
seldom asserted His claims ; He never argued
them. He simply manifested Himself, and such
as had eyes to see and hearts to understand
hailed Him as their Lord. He was ' His own
best evidence.'

Now if the evangelic portraiture be indeed
a faithful delineation of Jesus as He appeared
to His contemporaries, it should still

His por-
traiture, if
authentic,
should be
so now.
cast a spell upon those who approach it with open eyes and un-
prejudiced minds. It should silence
their doubt and compel their faith. The trouble
is that it is difficult in these days to approach it
thus. It is so obscured by traditional interpre-
tations that we can hardly see it in its simple
reality, its native beauty. Suppose that the
Gospels had been lost in early times, and were
discovered among those papyri which are being

unearthed from the Egyptian sand; or suppose that, like the old shoemaker in Tolstoy's story, *Where Love is, there God is also*, we had never seen them, and chanced upon a copy of them and read them for the first time: imagine the surprise, the wonderment, the fascination which would take possession of our minds. This experience is denied us; yet it is possible to attain it in some measure by resolutely dismissing the preoccupations alike of faith and of unbelief and contemplating without prejudice the picture which the Evangelists have painted, and allowing it to produce its inevitable impression upon our minds. And this is the experiment which we shall now essay. Let us survey the evangelic portraiture of Jesus as it stands before us, and consider what meets our eyes.

It is a singular picture, and the first peculiarity which arrests our attention is this—that it portrays *a sinless man*. The Evangelic Jesus is completely human, sharing all our common infirmities and restrictions. He suffers weariness, hunger and thirst, and pain. His knowledge is limited, and He confesses its limitations. Once He ap-

Survey of the evangelic portraiture:
1. A sinless man.

proaches a barren fig-tree, expecting to find fruit on it;* and again He says: 'Of that day or that hour knoweth no one, not even the angels in heaven, neither the Son, but the Father.'† And He is subject to temptation, being 'in all points tempted like as we are.'‡ Yet He is never worsted in the moral conflict. He is 'in all points tempted like as we are, yet without sin.' He passes through the daily ordeal stainless and blameless. He is among sinners, yet He is not of them.

The marvel of this representation is twofold. On the one hand, *Jesus claimed to be sinless.* He claims to be sinless. Searched by a multitude of curious and critical eyes, He issued His confident challenge: 'Which of you convicteth me of sin?'§ He often felt the pang of hunger, but never the sting of remorse; He was often weary, but He was never burdened by guilt; He abounded in prayer, but in His prayers there was no contrition, no confession, no cry for pardon. Not only before the world but before God He maintained His rectitude unfalteringly to the last. With the shadow of death closing

* Mark xi. 13. † Mark xiii. 32.
‡ Heb. iv. 15. § John viii. 46.

round Him, He could lift up His eyes to heaven
and say: 'I have glorified Thee on the earth: I
have finished the work which Thou gavest Me
to do. . . . And now come I to Thee.'*

This is a unique representation. A lively and
keen sense of sin is a constant characteristic of
the saints. It is related of Juan de Avila
(A.D. 1500-69) that, as he lay dying, the rector
of his college approached him and said: 'What
joy it must be to you to think of meeting the
Saviour!' 'Ah!' said the saint, 'rather do I
tremble at the thought of my sins.' Such has
ever been the judgment of the saints upon
themselves; but as for Jesus, no word of self-
condemnation ever passed His lips, no lamenta-
tion over indwelling corruption, no sigh for a
closer walk with God. It was not that He
closed His eyes to the presence of sin or made
light of its guilt. Renan, being asked what he
made of sin, answered airily: 'I suppress it!'
but that was not the manner of Jesus. His
assertion of the equal heinousness of the sinful
thought and the sinful deed † has immeasurably
extended the sweep of the moral law and
infinitely elevated the standard of holiness. No

* John xvii. 4, 13.   † Matt. v. 21-30.

soul has ever been so sensitive as His to the
taint of impurity; no heart has ever been so
oppressed by the burden of the world's guilt.
His presence was a rebuke and an inspiration;
and to this hour the very thought of Him has
the value of an external conscience. His spot-
less life is a revelation at once of the beauty
of holiness and of the hideousness of sin.

And not only does the Evangelic Jesus claim
to be sinless, but *His claim was universally
allowed*. It appears that the first to
His claim
allowed.   challenge it was the philosopher
Celsus, who puts an indefinite charge in the
mouth of his imaginary Jew—that Jesus 'did
not show Himself clear of all evils.' * His
enemies in the days of His flesh would fain have
found some fault in Him, and they searched
Him as with a lighted candle; yet they discovered only one offence which they might lay
to His charge; and they did not perceive that it
was in truth a striking testimony to His perfect
holiness. They saw Him mingling freely with
social outcasts, conversing with them and going

---

* Orig., *C. Cels.* ii. 41 : ἔτι δ' ἐγκαλεῖ τῷ Ἰησοῦ ὁ Κέλσος διὰ
τοῦ Ἰουδαϊκοῦ προσώπου ὡς μὴ δείξαντι ἑαυτὸν πάντων δὴ κακῶν
καθαρεύοντα.

to their houses and their tables; and they exclaimed: 'This man receiveth sinners, and
eateth with them!'* It would have been no
surprise to those Scribes and Pharisees had He
associated with sinners, being Himself a sinner.
Their astonishment was that He should do this,
being Himself, apparently, so pure; and their
outcry was a covert suggestion that, for all
His seeming holiness, He must be a sinner at
heart. The fault, however, lay not with Him
but with themselves. 'In judging the Lord for
receiving sinners,' says St. Gregory, 'it was
because their heart was dry that they censured
Him, the Fountain of Mercy.' They did not
understand that true holiness is nothing else
than a great compassion. Such was the holiness
of Jesus, and it was a new thing on the earth,
an ideal which the human heart had never
conceived. The Pharisee was the Jewish ideal
of a holy man, and it is an evidence of the
historicity of the Evangelic Jesus that He is so
widely diverse from that ideal.

It is very significant that our Lord's claim to
sinlessness should have been thus allowed and
unwittingly attested by those who were bent

* Luke xv. 2.

upon disproving it. Bronson Alcott once said
to Carlyle that he could honestly use the words
of Jesus, ' I and the Father are one.' ' Yes,' was
the crushing rejoinder, ' but Jesus got the world
to believe Him.'

Another arresting feature of the evangelic
portraiture is the claim which Jesus constantly
2 His unique   made and persisted in to the last—
relation   that *He stood in a unique relation
alike toward God and toward man.*

✝ He identified Himself with God. ' Therefore
the Jews sought the more to kill Him, because
                 He said God was His peculiar (ἴδιον)
toward God,   Father, making Himself equal to
God.'* ' He that receiveth you,' He says in
His charge to the Twelve,† ' receiveth Me, and
he that receiveth Me receiveth Him that sent
Me.' He sets Himself forth as greater than the
Prophets. They were ' slaves '; He is ' the Son,'
' the Heir.'‡ They had spoken of Him, and
seen His day afar off, and longed to see Himself; and He announces Himself as the fulfil-
ment of their prophecies and the satisfaction of

* John v. 18.   † Matt. x. 40.
‡ Matt. xxi. 34–38. Cf. Heb. i. 2.

their desire.* 'Beginning from Moses and all the Prophets, He interpreted unto them in all the Scriptures the things concerning Himself.' †

Moreover, He claimed to be at once the Saviour and the Judge of men. He had 'come to give His life a ransom for many'; ‡ He bade the weary and heavy laden toward men. come unto Him and find rest for their souls; § and He spoke of a day when 'the Son of Man shall come in His glory and all the angels with Him, and shall sit upon His throne of Glory, and before Him shall be gathered all the nations.' ‖ How tremendous His demands on His followers! He points to the dearest, tenderest, and most sacred of human relationships, and claims for Himself a prior devotion. 'He that loveth father or mother more than Me is not worthy of Me, and He that loveth son or daughter more than Me is not worthy of Me.'¶ 'If any man cometh unto Me and hateth not his own father, and mother, and wife, and children, and brethren, and sisters,

* Matt. xiii. 16, 17.   † Luke xxiv. 27.
‡ Matt. xx. 28.   § Matt. xi. 28, 29.
‖ Matt. xxv. 31, 32.   ¶ Matt. x. 37.

yea and his own life also, he cannot be My disciple.'*

It is not merely for God, nor yet merely for the Kingdom of Heaven, that He makes these stupendous claims: it is for Himself. Conceive such language on the lips of a Galilean peasant! On the lips of Socrates or Julius Cæsar it would have seemed the language of insanity, and would have been greeted with ridicule and reprobation. 'If Christ,' says S. T. Coleridge,† 'had been a mere man, it would have been ridiculous in *him* to call himself "the Son of man"; but being God and man, it then became, in his own assumption of it, a peculiar and mysterious title. So, if Christ had been a mere man, his saying, "My Father is greater than I" (John xv. 28), would have been as unmeaning. It would be laughable enough, for example, to hear me say, "My 'Remorse' succeeded, indeed; but Shakspeare is a greater dramatist than I." But how immeasurably more foolish, more monstrous, would it be for a *man*, however honest, good, or wise, to say, "But Jehovah is greater than I"!' Yet this was the language, the habitual language, of Jesus, and to those who

* Luke xiv. 26.   † *Table Talk*, May 1, 1823.

knew Him best and could judge most truly of the justice of His claims, it seemed natural and fitting on His lips. It was the blinded Jews who pronounced Him mad and sought to slay Him.*

Again, we observe *the words which the Evangelists ascribe to Jesus.* There are no words in the Scriptures or elsewhere comparable to them. They have a peculiar fragrance. They sparkle on the page like gems in a setting of base metal. We recognise instinctively where Jesus ceases and the Evangelist begins. My old teacher and friend, the late Professor A. B. Bruce, once told me how in the early days of his ministry it chanced that he was studying the miracle of the Healing of the Lunatic Boy, and he stumbled over the verse: 'Howbeit this kind goeth not out but by prayer and fasting.'† The mention of 'fasting' struck him as so alien from the spirit of Jesus. He referred to his Tischendorf, and what did he find? The verse is absent from the authentic text of St. Matthew, being an importation from the parallel narrative of St. Mark ;‡ and in the latter,

3 The words of Jesus: their distinction,

* John x. 20.   † Matt. xvii. 21.   ‡ Mark ix. 29.

furthermore, 'and fasting' is a gloss. Thus was his instinct justified. And the incident is an instance of a principle. The genuine sayings of Jesus are always self-attesting. They are distinguishable from counterfeits by simple inspection.*

And their vitality is perennial. They still throb, still kindle, still make our hearts burn within us, reminding us how He said :

their reality.

''The words that I have spoken unto you are spirit, and are life.'† 'The impression the Jesus of the Gospels produces on us,' says Hermann Kutter,‡ 'is one of unapproachable reality. As we listen to His striking words, we have no desire to study their grammatical construction or philosophical content—we are so amazed at their reality. Whether we understand them or not, we find ourselves asking if

---

* So Luke viii. 46 ascribes to Jesus the crude idea that the woman's touch drew power out of Him, as though His person were magnetic ; Mark v. 30 shows that it is no saying of Jesus but a comment of the Evangelic Tradition. Similarly Matt. xii. 40 is not only savourless but irrelevant, since the 'sign' to the Ninevites was the preaching of Jonah, not his adventure with the whale, of which they knew nothing ; and its absence from Luke xi. 29, 30 proves it a homiletic gloss. Cf. *The Days of His Flesh*, Introd., pp. xxx f.

† John vi. 63. ‡ *Soc. Democr.*, pp. 54 f.

they are not the keys of life's mysteries, and whether through them we shall not know the truth—the whole truth. . . . Whether spoken to the crowd or in the presence of the questioning Scribes, His words displayed the same judgment—there was nothing to retract, no mistake to correct.'

Another characteristic of the Evangelic Jesus is *His superiority to the distinctions of the world He lived in*—the distinctions of *class*, *sect*, and *nation*.

4. His superiority to contemporary limitations:

Class distinctions were strongly marked in Jewish society. At one extreme stood the 'Sinners,' the social outcasts; and at the other, condemning these and shunning the pollution of contact with them, the Pharisees, the holy men of Israel. With the former Jesus had much to do. They were the special objects of His solicitude, insomuch that He was nicknamed the 'Friend of Sinners';* and when the Pharisees blamed Him and accused Him of secret sympathy with sin, His defence was that He was the Physician of Souls, and therefore it was fitting that He should

(1) class: 'Sinners,'

* Matt. xi. 19.

take to do with the morally diseased: 'They that are whole have no need of a physician, but they that are sick.'*

He was the Friend of Sinners, but the singular fact is that He was the Friend of Pharisees too. Those 'holy men' were not all His enemies. Many of them, despite their prejudices, were earnest seekers after God, and they were well disposed to the Prophet of Galilee.† They would invite Him to their houses and their tables, and He gladly went and talked with them of the things of His Kingdom.‡

Pharisees,

Another despised class was womankind.§ It

* Matt. ix. 12. Cf. Diog. Laert., *Antisth.* vi. 6: ὀνειδι-ζόμενος ποτὲ ἐπὶ τῷ πονηροῖς συγγενέσθαι, καὶ οἱ ἰατροί, φησὶ, μετὰ τῶν νοσούντων εἰσὶν ἀλλ' οὐ πυρέττουσιν. Bunyan, *Jerusalem-Sinner*: 'Christ Jesus, as you may perceive, has put himself under the term of a Physician, a Doctor for curing of diseases: and you know that applause, and a fame, is a thing that physicians much desire. That is it that helps them to patients, and that also that will help their patients to commit themselves to their skill for cure, with more confidence and repose of spirit. And the best way for a doctor or physician to get themselves a name, is in the first place to take in hand, and cure some such as all others have given off for lost and dead.'

† Cf. Acts xv. 5.

‡ Cf. Luke vii. 36 ff., xi. 37 ff., xiv. 1 ff.

§ See *The Days of His Flesh*, p. 77.

was accounted unseemly for a Jew to salute a woman, or to converse with her openly, even if she were his wife or his daughter or his sister. Hence the surprise Women; of the disciples at the beginning of His ministry when, unfamiliar as yet with the Master's manner, they returned from Sychar and found Him sitting on Jacob's Well and 'talking with a woman.'* And in the Morning Prayer the men bless God for not making them Gentiles, slaves, women.† In Jesus womankind found a friend. Women were numbered among His disciples, and they proved nobly worthy of His grace, ministering to the necessities of His homeless condition ‡ and continuing faithful unto death. §

He was exempt also from the distinctions of sect. Think what it means that 'the Apostle

---

* John iv. 27, R.V.

† A similar sentiment is ascribed to Plato. Lact. III. xix. 17: 'Aiebat se gratias agere naturæ, primum quod homo natus esset potius quam mutum animal, deinde quod mas potius quam femina, quod Græcus quam barbarus, postremo quod Atheniensis et quod temporibus Socratis.' Cf. Plut., *Mar.* xlvi. 1. The sentiment was ascribed also to Thales (Diog. Laert. i. 33).

‡ Luke viii. 2.

§ Matt. xxvii. 55, 56; Mark xv. 40, 41; Luke xxiii. 48, 49.

choir' included Matthew the Taxgatherer and Simon the Zealot. The taxgatherers were

(2) sect:

Zealots and Tax-gatherers;

hated as agents of the Roman oppressor, and a Jewish taxgatherer was peculiarly odious. He was a hireling traitor to his country and his God. There was a wide gulf between the taxgatherers and the Zealots, those desperate patriots who had sworn relentless enmity against the imperial domination, and were ever kindling the flame of insurrection. Yet a taxgatherer and a Zealot met in brotherhood at the feet of Jesus. His heart had room for both.

Furthermore, He exhibited no national characteristics. And this is the more remark-

(3) nation-ality:

Jewish exclusiveness,

able inasmuch as He belonged to a nation notorious for its intense, exclusive, almost ferocious patriotism. The Jews were designated, not without justice, 'enemies of the rest of mankind,' and, according to the Roman satirist, they would not show the road to a wanderer unless he were a fellow-worshipper and would not guide thirsty travellers to a well unless they were circumcised.* A Jew was always recognisable. Could

* 1 Thess. ii. 15. Tac., *Hist.* v. 5: 'Apud ipsos fides

St. Paul ever have been mistaken for a Greek or a Roman ? Whatever sympathetic disguises he might assume, becoming 'all things to all men, that he might by all means save some,' he never ceased to be a Jew, a Hebrew of the Hebrews, proud of his nationality,* and overflowing with love for his people even while he pronounced their condemnation.†

It was otherwise with Jesus. He was purely human, and to this the Evangelists have borne a testimony all the more impressive that national it is undesigned. There were four sympathies of the distinct types of nationality at that Evangelists, period—the Jewish type, the Roman, the Greek, and the Alexandrian; and to these the four Gospels correspond. St. Matthew's is the Jewish Gospel, St. Mark's the Roman, St. Luke's the Greek, and St. John's the Alex- andrian. Each has interpreted Jesus for a race, and shown how He satisfied its peculiar need; but in so far each has belittled_Him. 'Moses

obstinata, misericordia in promptu, sed adversus omnes alios hostile odium.' Juv. xiv. 103 f. :

'Non monstrare vias eadem nisi sacra colenti,
Quæsitum ad fontem solos deducere verpos.'

* Phil. iii. 4–7.   † Rom. ix. 1–8.

for a people,' says Blaise Pascal; 'Jesus Christ for all men.' And this is the reason why there was need of four Gospels, that each nation might see Him as its own Saviour, and that humanity might recognise its unity in Him.

He was for all mankind. He bore no racial mark, insomuch that Renan, arguing from the name of the province, *Gelil haggoyim*, 'the Circle of the Gentiles,' that the Galileans were a mixed race, pronounces it impossible 'to ascertain what blood flowed in the veins of him who has contributed most to efface the distinctions of blood in humanity.' This is a perverse fancy, nevertheless it serves to emphasise an indubitable and truly remarkable fact. Jesus, though a Jew after the flesh,* was purely human. He recognised all the children of men as children of one Heavenly Father; He owned kinship with all, whether Jews or Gentiles, who did the Father's will; and He pronounced Jerusalem no whit more sacred than the mountain where the Samaritans worshipped. And all met in Him. He was— to employ an exquisite mistranslation—'the Desire of all nations,'† the Saviour for whom

universality of Jesus.

---

* Cf. Rom. ix. 5.   † Hagg. ii. 7.

the age-long hunger of the human heart had been an unconscious yearning, a blind groping.

One other feature of the Evangelic Jesus must be noted—*His singular attitude* 5 His detach-*toward the opinions of His day, His* ment from contemporary *absolute detachment from current* opinions; *theories.*

Apollonius of Tyana was a child of his age. He breathed its spirit and shared its beliefs; and as for his original ideas, though they seemed to his biographer pro- contrast with Apollonius of Tyana. digies of supernatural wisdom, they simply amuse us by their childishness. It is related, for instance, that on reaching the western coast of Spain he observed the phenomenon of the ocean's ebb and flow, so surprising to one accustomed to the tideless Mediterranean;* and he accounted for it by the theory that there are vast caverns at the bottom of the sea, and when the wind which fills these rushes out, it forces the water back upon the land ; then, when it returns like a great respiration, the water subsides.†

* Cf. the astonishment of the crews of Alexander (Arrian, *Anab.* vi. 19) and Cæsar (*De Bell. Gall.* vi. 29).
   † *Vit. Apoll.* v. 2.

There is nothing like this in the Gospels. 'One of the strongest pieces of objective evidence in favour of Christianity,' says

'One of the
strongest
pieces of
objective
evidence.'

the late Dr. G. J. Romanes,* 'is not sufficiently enforced by apologists. Indeed, I am not aware that I have ever seen it mentioned. It is the absence from the biography of Christ of any doctrines which the subsequent growth of human knowledge— whether in natural science, ethics, political economy, or elsewhere—has had to discount. This negative argument is really almost as strong as the positive one from what Christ did teach. For when we consider what a large number of sayings are recorded of—or at least attributed to—Him, it becomes most remarkable that in literal truth there is no reason why any of His words should ever pass away in the sense of becoming obsolete. . . . Contrast Jesus Christ in this respect with other thinkers of like antiquity. Even Plato, who, though some four hundred years before Christ in point of time, was greatly in advance of him in respect of philosophic thought, is nowhere in this respect as compared with Christ. Read the Dialogues,

* *Thoughts on Religion*, p. 157.

and see how enormous is the contrast with the Gospels in respect of errors of all kinds, reaching even to absurdity in respect of reason, and to sayings shocking to the moral sense. Yet this is confessedly the highest level of human reason on the lines of spirituality, when unaided by alleged revelation.'

Whatever its explanation, the fact stands that, so far as the record extends, there is nothing in the teaching of Jesus which implicated it with the notions of His day or—which is still more remarkable—has brought it into collision with the later discoveries of Science or Criticism. It was to the Book of Joshua and not to the Gospels that appeal was made in vindication of the Ptolemaic astronomy; when the Evolutionary Hypothesis was propounded, it was with the cosmogony of Moses and not with the teaching of our Lord that it seemed to conflict; and there is no pronouncement of His which prohibits Criticism from determining on proper evidence the date or authorship of the documents of the Old Testament.

It were, however, endless to exhibit all the wonder of the picture which the Evangelists have painted, and what we have seen is sufficient.

There are three results which have clearly emerged from our scrutiny.

The first is the superiority of the Evangelic Jesus to His biographers. He is not their creation. He always stands above them, and they look up to Him and seek to interpret Him. And frequently they misconstruc Him, thus unconsciously attesting His transcendence. 'Jesus himself,' says Matthew Arnold,* 'as he appears in the Gospels, and for the very reason that he is so manifestly above the heads of his reporters there, is, in the jargon of modern philosophy, an *absolute;* we cannot explain him, cannot get behind him and above him, cannot command him.' And it is very wonderful how the teaching of Jesus is ever in advance of the human intellect in its onward march. 'I venture to think,' says Dr. S. D. McConnell,† 'that Darwin and the martyrs of natural science have done more to make the word of Christ intelligible than have Augustine and the theologians. It is little less than marvellous, the

(1) the Evangelic Jesus superior to His biographers ;

---

* Preface to *Literature and Dogma.*
† *Evolution of Immortality*, pp. 135 f.

way in which the words of Jesus fit in with
the forms of thought which are to-day current.
They are life, generation, survival of the fit,
perishing of the unfit, tree and fruit, multiplica-
tion by cell growth as yeast, operation by
chemical contact as salt, dying of the lonely
seed to produce much fruit, imposition of a
higher form of life upon a lower by being born
from above, grafting a new scion upon a wild
stock, the phenomena of plant growth from the
seed through the blade, the ear, and the matured
grain, and, finally, the attainment of an individual life which has an eternal quality.' Thus
Science and Philosophy proclaim their inter-
pretations of the Universe, and sometimes these
seem subversive of things most surely believed ;
and, behold, it presently appears that they are
in truth no novel discoveries but principles
which have all along been lying unobserved
in the Christian revelation.

The Evangelic Jesus is independent of His
environment. It is impossible to analyse Him
and distinguish the influences which
went to the making of Him. He is (2) independent of
a debtor neither to the Jews nor to environment;
the Greeks. He is not a child of His age, else

He would have been, in every particular, other than He is. His is the one perfectly original and absolutely self-determined life in the history of mankind.

He stands for God. Apart from every metaphysical theory of His person, He has for all (3) stands time 'the value of God.' In Him for God. humanity finds evermore its highest conception of the character of God and His relation to the world. 'Religion,' says J. S. Mill,* 'cannot be said to have made a bad choice in pitching on this man as the ideal representative and guide of humanity; nor, even now, would it be easy, even for an unbeliever, to find a better translation of the rule of virtue from the abstract into the concrete, than to endeavour so to live that Christ would approve our life.'

Now, what must be said of this picture? Two answers have been given. One is that it is a Insufficient creation of some religious genius; explanations: and the other, that it is a product of the myth-forming genius of the primitive Church.

* *Three Essays on Religion*, pp. 254 f.

The former is, as we have seen, the answer of Green, who ascribes to St. John the 'final spiritual interpretation of the person of Christ,' which has 'fixed it in the purified conscience as the immanent God.' And it is the answer also of Pfleiderer. (1) a creation of religious genius;

His theory is that St. Paul was the creator of Christ, and this is the manner of his proof: he first ascertains from the recognised epistles what was the Apostle's conception of Christianity, and then he proceeds to demonstrate that it is reflected in the evangelic narrative.* It is not the Jesus of history that the Evangelists portray but the Christ of the Pauline theology.

A theory of this sort, however, simply creates a difficulty greater than that which it seeks to remove. When men make themselves a god, they always fashion him in their own likeness. The Ethiopians, said Xenophanes long ago in derision of the anthropomorphic deities of the Homeric poems,† made their gods black and snub-nosed like themselves; the Thracians made

---

* *Urchristenthum*, p. 520.

† Theodoret. *Græc. Affect. Cur.* iii. 780: Ξενοφάνης ὁ Κολοφώνιος τοιάδε φησίν·

ἀλλ' οἱ βροτοὶ δοκοῦσι γεννᾶσθαι θεούς,
τὴν σφετέρην δ' ἐσθῆτα ἔχειν φωνήν τε δέμας τε.

theirs blue-eyed and ruddy ; so, too, the Medes and Persians and the Egyptians also made theirs after their own image; and if horses and oxen had hands, they would make themselves gods in the likeness of horses and oxen. St. Paul was a Pharisee, and, had he been the creator of the Evangelic Jesus, he would have made Him in the likeness of a Pharisee. It is unthinkable, and contrary to all our knowledge of him, that he should have risen so far above himself as to conceive that transcendent ideal. And the issue is clear. If St. Paul were the creator of Jesus, then he was far greater than we have ever thought. To conceive so divine an ideal he must have been himself no less than divine, and it remains that we should transfer to him the adoration which we have paid to Jesus.

καὶ πάλιν·

ἀλλ' εἴ τοι χεῖρας εἶχον βόες ἠὲ λέοντες
ἢ γράψαι χείρεσσι καὶ ἔργα τελεῖν ἅπερ ἄνδρες,
ἵπποι μέν θ' ἵπποισι, βόες δέ τε βουσὶν ὁμοίας,
καί κε θεῶν ἰδέας ἔγραφον καὶ σώματ' ἐποίουν
τοιαῦθ' οἷόν περ καὐτοὶ δέμας εἶχον ὁμοῖον.

. . . τοὺς μὲν γὰρ Αἰθίοπας μέλανας καὶ σιμοὺς γράφειν ἔφησε τοὺς οἰκείους θεούς, ὁποῖοι δὲ καὶ αὐτοὶ πεφύκασιν· τοὺς δέ γε Θρᾷκας γλαυκούς τε καὶ ἐρυθρούς, καὶ μέντοι καὶ Μήδους καὶ Πέρσας σφισιν αὐτοῖς ἐοικότας· καὶ Αἰγυπτίους ὡσαύτως διαμορφοῦν πρὸς τὴν οἰκείαν μορφήν. Cf. Clem. Alex., *Str.* v. 109.

Neither can the Evangelic Jesus be a creation of 'the spontaneous productivity of the Christian spirit in the primitive Church.' Humanity cannot transcend itself. Surely scepticism has its credulity no less than faith when it is gravely maintained that so radiant an ideal dawned upon 'nearly the most degraded generation of the most narrow-minded race that the world has ever known, and made it the birthplace of a new earth.' * It arose in a land barren of wisdom and religiously bankrupt, and it has continued for more than sixty generations the wonder and inspiration of mankind. It must have been more than a dream : it must have been a manifestation. 'I cannot understand the history of the Christian Church at all, if all the fervent trust which has been stirred by faith in the actual inspirations of a nature at once eternal and human, has been lavished on a dream.' † That matchless Life, in which the Divine and the human meet, must have been actually lived upon the earth, else the ideal of it would never have entered into the heart of man.

(2) a product of the myth-forming genius of the Church.

* Hutton, *Theol. Ess.* viii. p. 290.
† *Ibid.*, p. 285.

And thus the Evangelic Jesus is Himself the supreme evidence at once of the historicity of the evangelic records and of His own Deity. No criticism can shake this sure foundation. It may be that the Gospels exhibit inaccuracies and inconsistencies—though it were well for such as love to dwell on these to lay to heart Rothe's warning against being so taken up with the sun-spots as to overlook the sun.* It may be that the Evangelists were liable to error and subject to the deflections of contemporary opinion and personal prejudice—though the more one studies their writings, the surer does one grow that untenable as every theory of Inspiration may and indeed must be, some singular aid was vouchsafed to those unlearned men who 'carried so much æther in their souls.'† It will hardly be disputed by any intelligent believer in the Deity of our Blessed Lord that He was imperfectly comprehended and incompletely represented by His

Conclusion: self-evidence of the Evangelic Jesus.

---

* *Stille Stunden*, p. 22 : 'Wer uber den Sonnenflecken die Sonne ubersieht, sieht der richtig?'

† Philostr., *Apoll. Tyan.* i. 33 : τοσοῦτον ἐν τῇ ψυχῇ φέρων αἰθέρα.

biographers—what human mind could perfectly comprehend or what human hand completely represent the vision of His glory? It is impossible to gainsay such contentions, but they may be the more cheerfully allowed inasmuch as they furnish no inconsiderable argument for the historicity of the evangelic narratives and the Deity of Him they tell of. The fact that Jesus is so manifestly 'above the heads of His reporters' is a conclusive proof that, when they wrote of Him, they were not dealing with imagination but relating in honest simplicity 'things which they had seen and heard.' And the very imperfection of their narratives is an involuntary testimony to His ineffable glory. After every deduction the Evangelic Jesus remains a wonderful portraiture. Blurred though it may be by the unskilfulness of the artists, it is still a picture limned in light of One fairer than the children of men; and if a picture painted by weak human hands be so transcendently beautiful, what must have been the glory of the Divine Original?

And thus we turn from the strife of criticism and, with quiet assurance, rest our souls on the

Evangelic Jesus as on a strong rock standing firm amid 'the removing of the things that are shaken.' It is the end of all controversy, the death of all doubt and fear, when He is recognised as the Incarnation of the Eternal God, the manifestation of the Unseen Father.

The end of all controversy.

> 'I say, the acknowledgment of God in Christ,
> Accepted by thy reason, solves for thee
> All questions in the earth and out of it.'*

It settles every dispute. Is it the existence of God that is disputed? Then Jesus is God manifest in the flesh, *Dei inaspecti aspectabilis imago.*† Is it immortality that is doubted? Then He has given us His word for it: 'If it were not so, I would have told you'; and He is the Lord of Eternity who left His glory to tell us what lies behind the shadow, that our hearts might be glad. Is it miracles that are in question? Then Jesus is Himself the Miracle of miracles. 'A *sinless* Christ,' says Professor Bruce,‡ 'is as great a miracle as a

* Browning, *Death in Desert.*
† Grotius on Col. i. 15.
‡ *Humiliation of Christ*, p. 208, n. 1.

Christ who can walk on the water.' In view
of the miraculousness of His person His
miraculous operations appear not merely
credible but inevitable. The wonder were if,
being what He was, He had not wrought
these.

In truth there is no certainty apart from Him.
'Other foundation,' says St. Paul,* 'can no man
lay than that which is laid, which is
Jesus Christ.' The objects of faith
do not admit of demonstration. 'All
first principles,' says Romanes,† 'even of scientific facts are known by intuition and not by
reason. No one can deny this. Now if there
be a God, the fact is certainly of the nature of
a first principle ; for it must be the first of all
first principles. No one can dispute this. No
one can therefore dispute the necessary conclusion that, if there be a God, He is knowable
(if knowable at all) by intuition and not by
reason.' So long as we rest on demonstration
we can never attain to more than probability,
and our faith lies at the mercy of each subtle
logomachist. That is a significant confession

The service
of Jesus to
faith.

* 1 Cor. iii. 11.
† *Thoughts on Religion*, p. 146.

which one of the persons in Cicero's *Tusculan Disputations* makes—that while he was reading Plato's splendid argument he felt sure of the Immortality of the Soul, but whenever he laid the dialogue aside his assurance slipped away from him.   And this is the priceless service that Jesus has rendered to our souls, which were made for God and are restless until they find rest in Him: He has lifted faith for ever out of the domain of reason into that of intuition, and has made it sure and abiding for every one who has eyes to behold His glory and a heart to understand His love.

THE EVIDENCE OF EXPERIENCE

'I heard certain say : "Unless I find it in the archives, I do not believe it in the Gospel." And when I said to them : "It is written," they answered me : "That is the question." For me, however, the archives are Jesus Christ, the inviolable archives His Cross and Death and His Resurrection and the Faith that is through Him ; wherein I would be justified by your prayer.'

ST. IGNATIUS, *Epistle to the Philadelphians*, viii.

V

THE EVIDENCE OF EXPERIENCE

IT must be confessed that the appeal to experience is a somewhat perilous expedient, nor should it be employed without much circumspection. It is Peril of appeal to experience. commonly no better than an *asylum ignorantiæ*, the refuge of hard-pressed enthusiasts and obscurantists when they are asked a reason concerning the hope that is in them, and find themselves unready to give an answer. 'It is absurd,' says St. Chrysostom,* 'that, while the physician contends with precision for his craft, and the currier, and the weaver, and every sort of craftsman, the Christian should allege that he cannot furnish a reason for his faith.' In its popular use the appeal to experience is too often a riot of unreason; and even in the hands of a philosopher it is apt to be nothing

* *In Ev. Joan. Hom.* xvi.

else than a reversion to the Protagorean *homo mensura*—'that man is the measure of all things: of the existent, that they exist; and of the non-existent, that they do not exist.'*
'He means by that,' says Socrates,† 'that, as everything appears to me, such is it to me; and, as it appears to you, such again is it to you.' And the consequence is that there is no objective certainty, nothing but the illusory impressions of the senses. There was, according to Protagoras, no soul beyond the senses, and all things alike were true; and he 'could know nothing about gods, either that they existed or that they did not exist; for there were many things that hindered knowledge—the lack of certainty and the brevity of the life of man.'‡

It is to this conclusion that the appeal to experience is apt to lead; nevertheless there is

Its legitimacy. a legitimate use of the argument. Indeed it is necessary; for apart from experience there can be no certitude, and it is the only final test. Was not Diogenes' appeal to experience reasonable and incontrovertible

* Diog. Laert. ix. 51: πάντων χρημάτων μέτρον ἄνθρωπος· τῶν μὲν ὄντων ὡς ἔστι· τῶν δὲ οὐκ ὄντων ὡς οὐκ ἔστι.

† Plat., *Theæt.* 151 E.   ‡ Diog. Laert., *ibid.*

when, unable to expose the fallacy of Zeno's paralogism of the impossibility of locomotion, he rose and walked? *Solvitur ambulando.*

The argument then is valid, if only its conditions be observed. And what are its conditions? The question resolves itself ultimately into the distinction Its conditions. between faith and superstition, and Romanes defines the criteria which differentiate these as 'the spiritual verification' and 'the moral ingredient.'* The spiritual verification is subjective, the moral ingredient is objective ; and where the latter is lacking, the former is invalid. It is told, for example, how an impostor, one Lacey of the sect of 'the Prophets,' once visited the Lord Chief-Justice Holt and demanded the release of a brother fanatic who had been thrown into Newgate for seditious talk. He announced himself as 'a prophet of the Lord God.' 'He has sent me to thee, and would have thee grant a *nolle prosequi* for John Atkins, His servant, whom thou hast sent to prison.' Lacey's revelation was, for him, a spiritual verification. The subjective condition was present, but what of the objective

* *Thoughts on Religion*, p. 139.

condition, the moral ingredient? It was lacking, and therefore the appeal to experience was disallowed. 'Thou art a false prophet,' was his lordship's reply, 'and a lying knave. If the Lord God had sent thee, it would have been to the Attorney General, for He knows that it belongeth not to the Chief-Justice to grant a *nolle prosequi*, but I, as Chief-Justice, can grant a warrant to lay a lying knave by the heels.'

The test of the argument then is pragmatic: it must work. The experience to which appeal

Pragmatism.

is made must be actual and verifiable, not subjective and personal but objective and demonstrable. Thus conditioned, it is the surest of all arguments, and it bears powerfully on the question of the historicity of the Evangelic Jesus.

You remember that principle which our Lord is reported in the Fourth Gospel to have

The appeal sanctioned by Jesus.

enunciated to the Jewish rulers when they were disputing about His teaching in the court of the Temple: *

'My teaching is not Mine, but His that sent Me. If any man willeth to do His will, he shall come to know (γνώσεται) of the teaching,

* John vii. 16, 17.

whether it be of God, or whether I speak from Myself.'

St. Augustine entirely misses the significance of this principle when, in his beautiful exposition of the Gospel, he thus explains it: No 'fool's 'Understanding is the reward of faith. experiment.' Never seek to understand in order that you may believe, but believe in order that you may understand.'* Our Lord is not recommending what Romanes terms the 'fool's experiment' of stifling one's doubt and blindly accepting an unintelligible creed in the hope of coming to believe it. On the contrary, He challenges honest investigation and proposes a method. And it is precisely the method which is pursued in every other domain.

It is the method of Science. The first step toward discovery is a theory; then follows the testing of the theory by the pheno- The method mena, and if these bear it out, it is of: forthwith established. It is mere loss (1) scientific of breath to reason about the theory. investigation; 'Do not think; try' that celebrated physician John Hunter was accustomed to say to his

* Cf. Anselm, *Proslog.* i. : ' Neque enim quæro intelligere, ut credam ; sed credo, ut intelligam.'

students ; meaning : 'Do not waste time on *à priori* discussion of the theory : put it to the test and ascertain the verdict of the facts.' *

Again, it is the method for the practice of Art. What was Rembrandt's counsel to his pupil Hoogstraten when the latter teased him with questions ? 'Try,' he said, 'to put well in practice what you already know. In so doing you will, in good time, discover the hidden things which you now inquire about.'

(2) the practice of Art;

And so in the domain of speculation. It was a shrewd observation of Dr. Samuel Johnson that 'so many objections might be made to everything, that nothing could overcome them but the necessity of doing something.' And Carlyle has proclaimed the same truth in his impassioned discourse on *The Everlasting Yea :* 'All speculation is by nature endless, formless, a vortex amid vortices : only by a felt indubitable certainty of Experience does it find any centre to revolve round, and so fashion itself into a system. Most true it is, as a wise man teaches us, that "Doubt of any sort cannot be removed

(3) speculative certainty.

* Romanes, *Thoughts on Religion*, p. 167.

except by Action." On which ground, too, let him who gropes painfully in darkness or uncertainty, and prays vehemently that the dawn may ripen into day, lay this other precept well to heart, which to me was of invaluable service:
X *"Do the Duty which lies nearest thee,"* which thou knowest to be a Duty! The second Duty will already have become clearer.'

In all these domains the principle is recognised; and when our Lord says: 'If any man willeth to do His will, he shall come to know of the teaching, whether it So in faith. be of God, or whether I speak from Myself,' He simply carries it into the domain of Religion with its peculiar perplexities, and insists that it be applied to these also. It is no 'fool's experiment' that He requires, no irrational acceptance of something unintelligible after the manner of St. Augustine's *crede ut intelligas.* His 'willing to do the will of God' corresponds in the domain of Religion to Rembrandt's 'trying to put well in practice what you already know' in the domain of Art, and Carlyle's 'doing the Duty which lies nearest thee, which thou knowest to be a Duty,' in the domain of Morals. He bids us assume the right attitude toward life with its manifold perplexities, toward our fellow-creatures, and toward the mysteries which encompass us. Face these insistent and ever-present actualities gently and faithfully; be patient; be brave; be kind; be large-hearted; seek the ends which you know to be best and highest. This is 'willing to do the will of God'; and the assurance is that in so doing we shall 'come to know of the teaching' of our Lord. We shall recognise its reasonableness; √ and it will fit in with our experience, and thus irresistibly attest its truth. It will prove itself the right key by opening the door.

This is the only and the infallible way to find the clue of the labyrinth and emerge into the **The clue of** broad light of day. It is the under-**the labyrinth.** lying reason of that wise counsel of Coleridge:* 'The best way to bring a clever young man who has become sceptical and unsettled to reason, is to make him *feel* something in any way. Love, if sincere and unworldly, will, in nine cases out of ten, bring him to a sense and assurance of something real and actual; and that sense alone will make him *think* to a sound purpose, instead of

* *Table Talk*, May 17, 1830.

dreaming that he is thinking.' Such is the method. It is like following the narrow and often hardly distinguishable track through a mountain-gorge. You are hemmed in on either hand by beetling crags, and you see no pass before you; but follow the track, and by and by you will gain the height, and the broad, sunlit landscape will break upon your view.

And it may be observed in passing that this is the principle which underlies the Reformed doctrine that the ultimate evidence for believers that the Holy Scripture is the Word of God is neither the judgment of the Church nor the force of reason, but the Testimony of the Holy Spirit in their own hearts. 'Though,' says Calvin,* 'one vindicate the Holy Word of God from the gainsayings of men, he will not thereby fix in their hearts the certitude which piety requires. Because religion seems to profane men to stand merely in opinion, they desire and demand that, lest they believe anything foolishly or lightly, it should be proved to them by reason that Moses and the Prophets spoke by divine inspiration (*divinitus*). But I

Cf. the Reformed Testimonium Spiritus Sancti.

Calvin.

* *Instit.* I. vii. 4.

answer that the testimony of the Spirit is superior to all reason. For, as God alone is a fit witness concerning Himself in His Word, so also the Word will not find faith in the hearts of men until it is sealed by the inner testimony of the Spirit.' 'This fact,' says Zwingli,* 'only pious minds know; for it does not depend on the disputation of man, but is seated most firmly in men's souls. It is an experience; for all the pious have experienced it. It is not a doctrine; for we see that very learned men are ignorant of a fact so very salutary. It is therefore in vain that we are so anxious for some because they will not receive the Word; but it will not be in vain that we should anxiously pray God that He may deign to bestow the grace of His Spirit and draw them to the recognition of His Word.'

Zwingli.

Such is the Argument from Experience; and now see how it bears upon the question of the historicity of the evangelic records.

Application to the evangelic problem:

They profess to depict Jesus as He appeared in the days of His flesh; but this is not their

* *De Vera et Falsa Religione Commentarius : De Ecclesia.*

whole claim.   For Jesus is not merely a historic personage.   He is the Living Lord, 'the same yesterday and to-day, yea and for ever';* and His promise to His disciples ere He left the world was that He would be 'with them all the days even unto the consummation of the age.'† As He was manifested in the days of His flesh, so is He evermore; and we know Him as He is by the memory of His manifestation.   And the Gospels are the record of that manifestation : we know it only through them.   Hence it follows that, if they be a true record, they must bring us into present and personal contact with the Living and Eternal Lord.   And this is the ultimate and decisive test of their truth : Do they fulfil that function ?   If they do, then their historicity is attested by experience.

the Evangelic Jesus the Living Lord ;

And they do.   In a letter from Paris in 1826 Erskine of Linlathen writes of his meeting with a little company of French Protes-tants.   'The characteristic of all these persecuted Christians is reality, and oh reality is everything !   They have found religion to be a thing worth suffering for, they have

present contact with Him through the Gospels ;

* Heb. xiii. 8.   † Matt. xxviii. 20.

found it a support under suffering; and they speak of it to others, not as of a logical system, but as of a new life, a heavenly strength, a very present help in trouble, and a medicine and a remedy for every evil under the sun.' Have we not all met believers of this sort?—people who could say with St. Paul:* 'I have been crucified with Christ; yet I live; and yet no longer I, but Christ liveth in me: and that life which I now live in the flesh I live in faith, the faith which is in the Son of God, who loved me, and gave Himself up for me.' For such Christ is an experience. They 'know Him whom they have believed,'† and they need no other evidence. It chanced to me once to witness an encounter between a sceptical physician and a young woman, poorly educated but taught of God. Regardless of the dictates of chivalry, he plied her with his infidel arguments. Her feeble attempts to answer these only exposed her to his mockery, and at last her eyes filled, and she said: 'Well, doctor, I cannot argue with you; but there is one thing I am sure of: I have found peace. Have you?' His face fell, and he kept silence and troubled her no more.

* Gal. ii. 20.　　　　† 2 Tim. i. 12.

Faith is impregnable when it is fortified by experience. To one who has passed through the Gospels into fellowship with the Living Saviour of whom they testify, it matters nothing though criticism denies their historicity. He believes in them because he believes in Jesus; and he believes in Jesus because he knows Him.

'Whoso hath felt the Spirit of the Highest
Cannot confound nor doubt him nor deny :
Yea with one voice, oh world, tho' thou deniest,
Stand thou on that side, for on this am I.'

Experience is personal and individual, yet it carries conviction even to those who are strangers to it. It was an alien experience, which he had never felt and could not understand, that first arrested John Bunyan and never let him go. He has told the story in his immortal autobiography : 'Upon a day the good providence of God called me to Bedford to work at my calling, and in one of the streets of that town I came where there were three or four poor women sitting at a door in the sun, talking about the things of God; and being now willing to hear their discourse, I drew near to hear what they said, for I was now a brisk talker in matters of religion : but they were far above my reach. Their talk was about a new birth, the work of God in their hearts, as also how they were convinced of their miserable state by nature. They talked how God had visited their souls with his love in the Lord Jesus, and with what words and promises they had been refreshed, comforted, and supported against the temptations of the devil. . . . And methought they spake with such pleasantness of Scripture language, and with such an appearance of grace in all they said, that they were to me as if they had found a new world—as if they were a people that dwelt alone, and were not to be reckoned among their neighbours.' The memory haunted him, and he could never rest until he had discovered the blessed secret and made the experience his own.

There is profound truth in Neander's maxim that 'it is the heart that makes the theologian,' *pectus est quod theologum facit.* A theologian should always be a preacher too. Experience is an essential *materia critica ;* and this is, to my mind, the fatal defect of much that is written in these days, that it is

Experience an essential materia critica.

purely academic and has never been submitted
to the test of experience. You will realise this
when you enter the blessed service of the Holy
Ministry, and are summoned to a chamber
where the shadow of death is falling. The
fitting words will not be lacking ; they will rise
unbidden to your lips—those immortal words
which, according to the Fourth Gospel, our
Lord spoke to His disciples when He was
bidding them farewell in the Upper Room :
'Let not your heart be troubled. In My
Father's house are many mansions ; if it were
not so, I would have told you : I go to prepare
a place for you. And if I go and prepare a
place for you, I will come again, and receive you
unto Myself, that where I am, there ye may be
also. Peace I leave with you, My peace I give
unto you : not as the world giveth, give I unto
you. Let not your heart be troubled, neither
let it be afraid.'* And as you repeat them, you
will see the dying lips murmuring them with
you, and a light, like the dawning of the glory
which shall be revealed, breaking on the wasted
face. In presence of such an experience much
that has been written on the Johannine problem

* John xiv. 1–3, 27.

will appear to you strangely futile. You will be very sure that, whatever criticism may say, those are the words of Jesus, as strong and fragrant at this hour as when they fell from His lips into the troubled hearts of the Eleven in the Upper Room.

It may, however, be objected that all this is nothing more than illusion. You remember

Not illusion.

the poet's picture of the hapless maiden whose lover was lost at sea, and who would not believe it but haunted the cliff, watching for his lingering sail on the far horizon and, as each night fell, still hoping for the morrow. Her faith was an illusion, benign yet unsubstantial.

> ' Mercy gave, to charm the sense of woe,
>   Ideal peace, that Truth could ne'er bestow.'

And the thought of Jesus has indeed brought peace to many a troubled heart, but may it not be an 'ideal peace,' born of a beneficent illusion ?

> ' While we believed, on earth he went,
>   And open stood his grave.
>   Men call'd from chamber, church, and tent ;
>   And Christ was by to save.

'Now he is dead! Far hence he lies
    In the lorn Syrian town;
And on his grave, with shining eyes,
    The Syrian stars look down.'

Carry the argument a little farther. An ideal can do much. It can inspire wonder, admiration, desire, worship. But there is an emotion, deeper, warmer, and sweeter, which no ideal can stir. An ideal cannot enkindle love. *The object of love: not an ideal,*

The only possible object of love is a person. And what manner of person? Not an ideal person. Is not this taught by the Greek fable of Pygmalion? His Galatea was indeed his own crea- *only a person, real, living, near.* tion, but it was not until his ideal took visible shape that it enkindled love in his heart, and the responsive marble breathed and moved. It is impossible to love an ideal person; nor is it possible to love one who, though real, is merely historic. We cannot love Moses or Isaiah or St. Paul or St. Augustine or Martin Luther or John Knox or Sir Walter Scott. Nor can we love even a contemporary personage whom we know only afar off. A king has the reverence and loyalty of his subjects, but it is his kinsfolk and friends that love him.

The object of love, then, is a person, and a person who is real, living, and near. There is only One 'whom not having seen we love.' * And there is no love comparable to the love which He has inspired in the breasts of the children of men. Think of St. Francis of Assisi. It was a vision of Jesus that transformed him; and it is told how 'from that hour his heart was wounded and melted at the remembrance of the Lord's Passion.' † Think of St. Thomas Aquinas. 'Thou hast written well of Me, Thomas,' said the voice from the Crucifix as he bowed in prayer: 'what recompense dost thou desire?' 'None other,' answered the saint, 'than Thyself, O Lord.' Think of St. Bernard of Clairvaux:

The love of Jesus:

St. Francis of Assisi,

St. Thomas Aquinas,

St. Bernard of Clairvaux.

'Jesus, the very thought of Thee
    With sweetness fills my breast;
But sweeter far Thy face to see,
    And in Thy presence rest.

---

* 1 Peter i. 8.

† 'Ab illa hora vulneratum et liquefactum est cor ejus ad memoriam Dominicæ passionis.'

'O Hope of every contrite heart,
    O Joy of all the meek,
To those who fall how kind Thou art!
    How good to those who seek!

'But what to those who find? Ah! this
    Nor tongue nor pen can show;
The love of Jesus what it is
    None but His loved ones know.'*

Jesus, Thou Joy of loving hearts,
    Thou Fount of Life, Thou Light of men,
From the best bliss that earth imparts
    We turn unfilled to Thee again.†

---

   *   'Jesu dulcis memoria
    Dans vera cordi gaudia:
    Sed super mel et omnia
    Ejus dulcis præsentia.

    'Jesu spes pœnitentibus,
    Quam pius es petentibus,
    Quam bonus te quærentibus,
    Sed quid invenientibus?

    'Nec lingua valet dicere,
    Nec litera exprimere:
    Expertus potest credere
    Quid sit Jesum diligere.'

   †   'Jesu dulcedo cordium,
    Fons vivus, lumen mentium,
    Excedens omne gaudium,
    Et omne desiderium.

'Our restless spirits yearn for Thee,
    Where'er our changeful lot is cast,—
Glad when Thy gracious smile we see,
    Blest when our faith can hold Thee fast.' *

Samuel
Rutherfurd,

Think of Samuel Rutherfurd:

'Oh! Christ He is the fountain,
    The deep sweet well of love!
The streams on earth I've tasted,
    More deep I'll drink above.
There to an ocean fulness
    His mercy doth expand,
And glory, glory dwelleth
    In Immanuel's land.'

John Newton.   ## Think of John Newton:

'How sweet the name of Jesus sounds
    In a believer's ear!
It soothes his sorrows, heals his wounds,
    And drives away his fear.

'It makes the wounded spirit whole,
    And calms the troubled breast;
'Tis manna to the hungry soul,
    And to the weary rest.'

---

*   'Quocunque loco fuero,
    Mecum Jesum desidero:
    Quam lætus cum invenero?
    Quam felix cum tenuero?'

Was there ever a love like this—this passion of desire, this ecstasy of devotion? And its object is Jesus—the Evangelic Jesus, for He is the only Jesus whom we *Conclusion.* know. See, then, what follows. The Evangelic Jesus cannot be a mere ideal; for an ideal cannot enkindle love. He is a historic person, and He lived among men as the Evangelists have portrayed Him. But He is more than that. It is impossible to love one who is remote from us, and has never been in present and personal contact with us; and therefore Jesus is more than a historic person who dwelt in Palestine long ago. He is the Living Lord, the Eternal Saviour, who was manifested, according to the Scriptures, in the days of His flesh and still, according to His promise, visits the souls that put their trust in Him and makes His abode with them.

Here lies the supreme and incontrovertible evidence of the historicity of the Gospels. The final decision rests not with the critics but with the saints; and their verdict *The final verdict of the saints* is unanimous and unfaltering. They know the Divine Original, and they attest the faithfulness of the portrait.

A LATIN HYMN

The Sighs of St. Aloysius

O CHRIST, Love's Victim, hanging high
   Upon the cruel Tree,
What worthy recompense can I
   Make, mine own Christ, to Thee?

All my life's blood if I should spill
   A thousand times for Thee,
Ah, 'twere too small a quittance still
   For all Thy love to me.

My sweat and labour from this day,
   My sole life let it be,
To love Thee aye the best I may,
   And die for love of Thee.

INDEXES

I

NAMES AND SUBJECTS

II

PASSAGES OF SCRIPTURE

UNWIN BROTHERS, LIMITED, THE GRESHAM PRESS, WOKING AND LONDON.